Game Shooting

Also by John Marchington

Your Book of Photographing Wild Life
Shooting – A Complete Guide for Beginners
An Introduction to Bird and Wildlife Photography
(with Anthony Clay, A.R.P.S.)
Sportsman's Bag

Game Shooting

Management & Economics

John Marchington
with photographs by the author

Faber and Faber
3 Queen Square London

First published in 1976
by Faber and Faber Limited
3 Queen Square London WC1
Printed in Great Britain by
Latimer Trend & Company Ltd Plymouth
All rights reserved

ISBN 0 571 10943 8

DEDICATION

To those friends whose kindness has given me so much pleasurable sport; and in particular, to Peter Bruckmann, Dick Clarke, David Hewetson-Brown, Peter Neale, Anthonie Stilgoe, John Wardell and the Wells family.

© 1976, John Marchington

Contents

Illustrations   *page* 7

Acknowledgements   8

Foreword   9
by Charles Coles, Director of the Game Conservancy

Introduction   11
Economics and management – an interpretation of game shooting – the plight of the sport – the history of game shooting – the Game Conservancy and other organisations

Chapter 1   Forming a New Shoot   18
Ambitions and costs – the burdens of an organiser – profit and sport – the ground and the members – a hypothetical shoot – the search for economies – insurance – VAT

Chapter 2   The Ground   26
The impossibility of perfection – how to search – on taking the initiative – assessing the ground – the importance of cover – the arithmetic of drives – trespass and poaching – hidden problems – negotiating the rent – the lease – and the small print – improving the ground – advice from the Game Conservancy

Chapter 3   The Economics of Driven Shooting   36
The pressure of inflation – where the money goes – possible savings – keepering efficiency – utilising ground potential – economies through large-scale rearing, purchasing, etc. – monitoring released birds – vehicle economy – saving on beaters – selling the bag

Chapter 4   The Organisation of Driven Shooting   44
On firm control – forming the team – and vetting them – insurance – safety – subscriptions and substitute Guns – half Guns – sharing the work load – neighbourly relations – shooting dates – planning the drives – stops – averaging the sport – outside days – bag adjustment – the ladies – details on the day – shooting lunches – tipping – rain

Contents

Chapter 5 On a Lesser Scale 59

A new wind through game shooting – the road to major economies – part-time keepers – the arithmetic of buying in poults – rearing – poaching – scaling down in all departments – hypothetical figures – 'self-help' syndicates – management policy and general details – garden rearing – organising shooting days – practical examples

Chapter 6 Keepers and Keepering 73

Cost effectiveness – finding a keeper – supervision – keepering and the law – modern rearing techniques – releasing – foxes – preventing 'straying' – feeding techniques – automatic feeders

Chapter 7 Rough Shooting 80

A definition – the ground – leases – the size of the team – simple improvements – rearing – pre-shoot preparations – wet areas – insurance

Chapter 8 Grouse, Partridge and other Game 86

Grouse and their reasonable future – partridges and their less certain future – partridge statistics of the past – the Game Conservancy partridge research project – snipe – and habitat improvement – woodcock – ptarmigan – hares

Chapter 9 Of General Concern 93

Safety in changed circumstances – 'poaching' – planning for safety – placing quality before quantity – and how to achieve it – contemporary sporting agencies – the future for shooting

Appendix A 100
A schedule of Game Conservancy Booklets

Appendix B 101
A specimen letter setting out the basis of syndicate membership

Index 103

Illustrations

All photographs, including that on the jacket, were taken by the author

between pages 32 and 33

1. Lunch break on a grouse moor   2. A cock pheasant   3. Ptarmigan changing into summer plumage   4. A red grouse in flight   5. Hand feeding pheasants   6. Old-style rearing field   7. A large modern brooder   8. End of a prolific day

between pages 68 and 69

9. A high pheasant   10. Norfolk beaters waiting for the whistle   11. A team of springer spaniels   12. A simple feed point   13. Unpaid beaters   14. A knowledgeable man and his dog   15. Shoot organiser at work   16. Snipe and good habitat   17. 'Coffee-housing'   18. Game-cart

Acknowledgements

My thanks are due to the following: firstly, and as always, to my wife Janet, who has not only typed the manuscript, but observed and corrected my numerous grammatical errors; to Charles Coles, Director of the Game Conservancy, for so kindly finding the time, in his busy life, to write the Foreword; to Wilson Stephens, Editor of *The Field*, for his willingness to listen to my ideas, and his skill at detecting the flaws; and, finally, to the Editors of *The Field* and the *Shooting Times* for permission to reproduce some of my photographs which have previously appeared in their publications.

Foreword

Few books on game management have actually taken a shoot apart, and looked carefully at the economics of running it. John Marchington's new book, which is greatly concerned with costs, has come just at the right time – particularly for the thousands of syndicates who have recently been wondering how to effect savings without unduly reducing their sport. The author also gives much good practical advice on many aspects of shoot management, of which he himself has considerable experience. It is clear, thankfully for his readers, that he has learned the hard way: run syndicates where all has not always gone smoothly, employed keepers – good and bad – and himself reared hundreds of pheasants in his back garden.

Although he writes with all the delightful charm and understanding of a true countryman, he is never *just* bemused by misty mornings and the sharp smell of bog mint, for he is also a researcher with a very inquiring mind. However well he knows his subject from his experience as a sportsman – gained between the Home Counties and the Hebrides – he always delves further into the technical facts concerned with management and conservation. His recommendations are therefore accurate and always workable. In an earlier book (*Sportsman's Bag*) I remember him explaining clearly and convincingly the correct arguments about woodpigeon control, over-shooting, food shortages and so on. Others stuck firmly to the current safe and hoary old wives' tale. They were wrong.

Incidentally, although he deals mainly with what he calls shoots 'on a lesser scale' I can think of some shoots on the 'grand scale' which would benefit by a number of his suggestions. Cutting corners is not always a good policy in shoot management, but equally there are still too many estates that are old-fashioned – perhaps shielded from change – and where, when economies are made, they are often the wrong ones. Sadly in many ways – for the really well-run shoots invariably embrace beautiful stretches of countryside, employ dedicated staff and show superbly exciting sport – such large estates are cutting back and all too many disappearing altogether.

It is not just the overspill of pheasants that the less fortunate neighbours will miss, but the proximity of well-planned habitat, enough food for the wild game, a farming programme that takes wildlife into account and the nearby oasis of clean ground, without hoards of pests and predators to live off the game surplus that the owner and his staff has created with skill.

In the years ahead more shooting will undoubtedly have to be conducted on the 'lesser scale'. This need have no effect on the quality of the birds – only on the quantity shot and the number of miles we walk. Each such smaller shoot can go a long way towards becoming a parcel of good game country, and John Marchington's book will be of the greatest value in helping to make it so.

The author is also a photographer of great experience; his writing always lucid and amusing – colourful enough, in fact, for shooting wives to enjoy as well. Not forgetting that in one of his chapters the author says, 'Given a sensible and obedient wife . . .'

I can see her now ploughing onward through shoulder-high brambles, resolutely following the faithful spaniel, and perhaps carrying a magazine of cartridges on her head!

Charles Coles
Game Conservancy, Fordingbridge

Introduction

Writing in 1833, Colonel Peter Hawker, perhaps the most famous of all shooting men, in a preface to his classic *Instructions to Young Sportsmen*, said, 'So much, indeed, has been published, by more able writers, on field sports of every description, that little remains to be said on the subject.' In spite of this comment he then went on to say a great deal more, and subsequent writers have followed his example by producing many books, containing millions of words, on the sport. This would be more understandable if shooting had seen great changes during the last century or so, but it has not. All has not stood still, but sportsmen of the last century, taken wildfowling or to a driven pheasant shoot, would not feel lost. Changes of detail, yes, but nothing that a couple of good volumes could not encompass.

This being so, I must first explain my temerity in believing that this book makes a useful contribution to the literature of shooting.

Readers will quickly discover that it offers little of the conventional advice on such matters as how to hit curling pheasants, or the best techniques for predator control. So many practical men have acquired these skills, and so many excellent writers have detailed them, that there is little justification for serving the same dish under the sauce of a different cover and title.

Instead I am concerned with the somewhat neglected aspects of economics and management.

Until recently the economics of game shooting was a fairly simple matter, at least for those shooting men who merely participated rather than organised. Even the organisers had relatively few problems, for the pattern of expenses only varied slowly. Now heavy inflation is seriously affecting many aspects of shooting, and particularly game shooting. One of my principal objects has been to examine the various ways of combating inflation, either by practising economies, or by reorganising the shoot.

To talk of management, with its high-pressure business connections, in the same breath as the entirely non-commercial and pleasurable activity of shooting, arouses an automatic resistance. None of us wants to think of our sport in such terms. However, there are pressing reasons why we must, and this applies as much to a small rough shoot as to a grand syndicate. Good management not only increases sport and reduces costs, but goes a great deal further. It reduces the risk of accidents; eliminates the irritations created by bad organisation; ensures hot drinks on cold days; and a hundred and one other factors which make the difference between good days and quickly forgotten ones. Good management will also pay regard to other less obvious matters – for example, the legal relationship between the organiser and the other Guns in such matters as a failure of the rearing programme, or an unsafe shot harming someone.

Management, however, is not all detail. A good organiser will pay close regard to detail, but will always have central in his mind a clear picture of what he is trying to achieve and the resources at his command. Nor is this need for clear thinking confined to larger shoots – the point can be brought home quite sharply to an ambitious rough shoot which runs out of winter feed in November as a result of spending too much on rearing in July!

These, then, are the aspects which are the dominant themes of this book.

Having explained why this book has been written, I now come to who it is written for. It is not, and I stress this, written simply for the betterment of formal driven shooting. Game shooting, in my interpretation, is the pursuit of all forms of game by any sporting shooting means. Many previous books have treated game shooting as driven shooting and left lesser forms to be covered by books on rough shooting. This has ignored the many in-between shoots with numerous permutations of part-time keepers – no keepers – Guns that sometimes act as beaters or keepers – and other arrangements to contrive sport at modest cost. Under inflation these forms of shoots are likely to grow more common, and I devote a chapter to their possibilities and problems. Even a couple of friends with a small rough shoot, where they release a few birds and carry out a little winter feeding, are game shooters, and often more so in the spirit of the sport than the Gun in a large syndicate.

In short, therefore, this book is written for everyone who shoots game at any level; but it is principally for those who, usually for no reward, assume the responsibility of formulating and organising the shoot. I hope that, whether the individual is managing a high-powered syndicate or is the ideas man behind a small rough shoot, he will find some worth while suggestions in this book. Even the more passive sportsman should find it useful reading, if only to show him how much thought and effort goes into putting a goodly number of fast, high pheasants over the Guns. For those planning to form a new shoot, particularly the majority who will now face financial problems, the whole book should be useful, but for those planning to improve an existing shoot, or institute economies, the early chapters can be missed.

Introduction

As I stressed earlier I am not trying to impart detail already well known – essentially we know what we should do, and the problem is deciding on the priorities and then carrying them out as efficiently as possible.

Certain difficulties presented themselves in the composition of this book. Firstly, the decline of the partridge means that, for many men, game shooting consists almost exclusively of pheasants, and to be realistic long sections have had to be devoted to pheasants alone. In compensation, there is a chapter given to other game.

Secondly, comes the problem of changing money values, for whatever figures I give will be out-dated in months rather than years. Where possible I have talked in relative terms rather than actual figures. Where it is not I hope readers will be able to make mental adjustments.

Next, came the difficulty of writing at all times for all levels of shoots. The chapter 'On a Lesser Scale' is intended for the smaller shoots, but I hope such organisers will find a great deal of help elsewhere in the book.

Finally, I found myself uncertain of what collective name to give those creative sportsmen who are the shoot owners, syndicate managers, syndicate captains and the like. In the end I settled on shoot organisers, for this is what they are.

Although few readers will be unaware of the economic problems which face both individuals and the country, it is worth while recording the situation now, so a future generation can see the difficulties shooting faced in the seventies. At this moment inflation is running at more than 20 per cent per annum, and wages for many workers are increasing at 30 per cent. On the Stock Exchange many shares have fallen to a quarter of their previous values, and some of the largest and best known firms in the country have either collapsed or are in serious difficulties. In my personal experience many men, soundly based, with whom I have had business dealings for years, have either gone bankrupt or retired prematurely. The middle classes (who, according to Richard Jefferies, writing in the last century, were the very people who gave birth to the shooting syndicates) are the hardest hit, and particularly the self-employed whose costs leap upwards, but have little power to demand higher remuneration.

The effect, in the world of shooting, is that not for many years have so many syndicates had vacant Guns; ground is far more freely available to rent; and, most unfortunately, some keepers are losing their jobs. All around one hears that X will not be rearing birds this year, and that Y is cutting back severely. On the very day I write this I spoke with the game farmer from whom I purchase day-old pheasants. He was depressed and worried, with orders well down on the previous year and many of the shoots he normally supplied disbanded. The fact is that everyone who shoots game has the quality of his sport threatened, and this applies as much to the small rough shoot as the large private owner, for the large shoots are the reservoirs that maintain the pheasant population of the country generally. Of course, shooting will survive – it always will as long as there are wild creatures to be outwitted and men retain the hunting instinct – but my object is to suggest ways in which it can be made to survive at the best level. For some very busy men, whose participation has been limited to passing over a cheque and turning up on alternate Saturdays, then perhaps it is, at least for the time being, the end of an era. If they cannot pay more they must accept less. For others, unable to pay more, the maintenance of their standard of sport may require them to take a personal hand in some of the day-to-day work of the shoot. It is difficult to see this as an altogether bad development. For years I have reared several hundred pheasants in my own garden and it is a satisfying task.

In the state of the world as I write, with famine and misery on massive scales, I should, perhaps, feel slightly uneasy at devoting a book to a pleasurable activity. I am not. The pursuit of pleasure does not necessarily mean we are insensitive to the plight of others – merely practical. I forget who wrote it, but I like the observation that we must all find our own quiet corner in the garden of life, and cultivate it to the best of our ability. Nor am I defensive about the sport of shooting as an ethical activity. There is no point in restating the defence to those who already know it but, properly conducted, we have no need to feel sensitive about our sport. Not the least of our strengths is that, in a world whose capacity to produce food is rapidly being over-taken by the mouths requiring feeding, we produce a valuable food source which, at least in the case of syndicates, is subsidised by the sportsmen.

Game shooting has a rich heritage and before dealing with the present and the future, a brief look at the past is interesting. Up to the middle of the seventeenth century, men had shot for food rather than pleasure, but King Charles II and his courtiers, whilst exiled in Europe, experienced shooting flying birds, and brought the new-found sport back to this country. By the beginning of the eighteenth century it was well established, but only among the wealthy, and in the form of rough shooting. Over the next hundred years most improvements took place with the guns rather than the form of sport, with the development of the flint gun reaching its peak under Joe Manton. It was not until the early years of the nineteenth century that rearing on a large scale began, and in 1836, *Gamonia or the art of preserving game* was published, and landowners began planting coverts specifically for shooting. Meanwhile the invention of percussion ignition in 1807 ousted the flintlock and made the rapid showing of large numbers of birds practical; although most shooting was still carried out over pointers and setters. In 1851 the first breech-loaders of French origin appeared in Britain, and the English makers were quick to adapt and improve them so that when, in the last half of the century, rearing and driving took place on a much larger scale, adequate weapons were available. An illustration of the increased scale of shooting in the nineteenth century is given by comparing the results of Colonel Peter Hawker and Lord Ripon (although not strictly fair, as Lord Ripon had the entrée to some of the best estates in the country). In the fifty-one years between 1802 and 1853 Colonel Hawker shot 575 pheasants, yet in the twenty-eight years between 1867 and 1895 Lord Ripon bagged 111,190. Ripon's results were obtained at a time when the landed gentry of the country had reached their peak of affluence, and fashionable shooting house parties were an important part of the social calendar.

Although it is easy to be critical of this era, both because of the vast bags and the social privilege involved, it was an interesting facet of shooting history. The period is well documented by a number of shooting books, but the majority were written by sportsmen who, naturally, were the privileged minority, and rather took for granted aspects which we now find exceptional. In this context the full atmosphere is perhaps better judged by one of the few writers who viewed the scene from the other side.

Tommy Turner was the Head Keeper on the great Elveden estate, and in his book, *Memoirs of a Gamekeeper*, he dealt with the period from 1868 to 1953. This is a book worth tracking down, for the tale of the rise and subsequent decline of Elveden is not only a fascinating social document, but an illustration in miniature of the fortunes of Britain. Some of the sporting statistics leave me awed. Lord Iveagh bought the estate in 1894 and in the first season the total bag was 24,731, including 15,100 pheasants. In one day alone seven Guns killed over 1,500 head. More men were engaged for the Game Department until, eventually, there was a permanent staff of seventy; a fact which contrasts rather vividly with the struggles of present-day syndicates to afford a single-handed keeper. In some years more than 20,000 pheasants were reared, and on shooting days the many beaters wore white smocks with red collars and red-banded hats. There were over a hundred beaters and pickers-up involved on 5 November 1912, when the British record for a mixed bag of pheasants and partridges was established. Three thousand, two hundred and forty-eight head were killed by five Guns who included King George V, and in the three days of 5, 6 and 7 November these Guns killed 7,885 head.

In general these fantastic bags ended with the First World War, but on 6 November 1923 a new record for partridges was established with 835.

Politically it is now considered wrong that the master/servant relationship that existed between the owners and staff of the big estates should endure. When, however, we look at the modern equivalents in the form of large commercial enterprises, and the evident bitterness between management and men, it is difficult to believe that all was entirely wrong with a relationship in which Lord Iveagh could write the Foreword to his Keeper's book and conclude, 'I am grateful to my old friend for many things, and not least for the manner in which he has gathered together so much of a past which includes the whole of my life.'

Leaving my central theme for a moment, Turner's book helps to remind us of how the problem of inflation is a very recent evil. He describes how, in 1868, married men were paid 10s a week. Recently a friend showed me the records of his grandfather's Sussex shoot, and in 1930 the Keeper was paid 25s a week. At the present rate of inflation this percentage increase will be achieved in nearer five years than sixty-two!

The social upheaval brought about by the First World War produced the various forms of heavy taxation which contributed towards the end of the great landed estates with large staffs. Between the two World Wars formal driven shooting relied mainly on two forms of participants – the syndicates and the private owners, the latter usually owner/farmers, where much of the cost was lost in the farming operations. Now the position is much the same, except that the syndicate members, finding their subscriptions from taxed income, are under heavy financial pressure.

Quite where we go in the future defies accurate analysis, although Chapter 9 attempts some conclusions. All that is certain is that the responsibility for maintaining the standards of the sport of shooting depends on us. Whether or not we maintain quantity is, in the long run, of no great importance. What does matter is that we continue to insist on strict sporting standards, but such monstrosities as five-shot repeating guns and 'instant' pheasants are so distastefully regarded that I have no fear for the foreseeable future.

At this point I am anxious to pay tribute to the work of the Game Conservancy, and in particular express my thanks to its Director, Charles Coles, for his help and advice; not least for kindly writing the Foreword. The Conservancy was born of purely commercial considerations in 1932. Cartridge sales had fluctuated widely, from season to season with the varying partridge population, and in an effort to stabilise both production and sales the ICI Game Research Station

Introduction

was established. All the services were free, and at the peak the staff were making some 1,000 shoot visits a year, and gave away over a million brochures. After the war the title changed to the Eley Game Advisory Station, and in 1969 ICI decreed that the organisation must become national. In effect this meant the Conservancy must become self-supporting within a reasonable time, and this they are striving to achieve. The work of the Conservancy is of the utmost importance to the sport, not least because the staff are all practical shooting men and not just theoretical scientists. One of the reasons I have not attempted detailed instruction on many aspects is that so much is already covered by the excellent series of Game Conservancy booklets. These are so comprehensive that I list them in Appendix A on page 100. The services of the Conservancy are available to all shooting men, whether members or not, but I think most readers will agree there is a moral obligation upon everyone, except the most impecunious, to join and support their work.

The other organisation to which membership is morally obligatory is the British Field Sports' Society, which works for the political defence of field sports. By the very nature of its work not much is heard of its activities, and shooting men tend to ignore it until some threat to the sport develops, when membership jumps. This is very wrong and the Society obviously requires regular support at all times.

WAGBI, once concerned purely with wildfowlers, has in recent years extended its interest and activities to all forms of shooting, and now speaks with a very powerful voice in support of the sport. It, too, deserves the support of all shooting men.

It can be argued that, in urging readers to belong to three separate organisations, I call for an unreasonable annual financial outlay. I disagree. The cost of this comprehensive support is small when viewed as a percentage of most men's annual expenditure on shooting. In return for this modest outlay sportsmen receive the dedicated efforts of many knowledgeable men, some working in an honorary capacity, to further all aspects of the sport; and, most important of all, these organisations are our only shield against political interference.

The shooting scene, at this time, is neither cheerful nor settled, and, as with the national problems, the need is not to sit and bemoan our difficulties but to do something practical about them. I cannot think of any group of people more likely to support this view than the shooting community, and therefore submit this brief work in the hope that it will offer both advice and encouragement.

John Marchington
Great Bookham 1975

I

Forming a New Shoot

As is obvious from the title the purpose of this chapter is to give advice to men thinking of forming a shoot. Reading it is not, however, necessarily a waste of time for those already running a shoot, for some basic re-thinking on what they are trying to achieve, and how, may be useful in solving the problems currently besetting all game shooters. Nor are these thoughts only intended for men planning a large-scale syndicate or private driven shoot. Game shooting, as I stressed in the Introduction, is shooting game at all levels and a small rough shoot, in which the work as well as the expertise is shared by a few companions, can call for much planning if it is to achieve optimum results.

This said, however, the more ambitious your plans the more forethought is required, for whilst failure in a rough shoot means fewer pheasants in the bag, at the other extreme it can be very expensive – and also personally embarrassing if you have assumed responsibility.

You may reasonably ask why, at a time when shooting is facing great financial pressure and many shoots are being forced to break up, I feel the need exists for advice on forming new ones. It is because for the first time for many years the opportunity exists to lease reasonable ground. It has been well-nigh impossible for the man without contacts in the farming world to find ground at a sensible rent, unless, that is, it has been so distant as to make travel impractical. Now the position is much improved, but it is unlikely to remain so and those who do not grasp the chance may find it has gone for a long time.

If you are not to drift into a situation which turns out to be far from your original intentions you must firmly define the scope of your ambitions, and secondly make a realistic appraisal of the costs. What are your motives? Do you wish to be the powerhouse of a model shoot producing a large annual bag, or is happiness for you limited to working out hedgerows with a couple of friends and a spaniel? Do you believe that shooting means friendly, happy people and that 'coffee-housing', the sin against which so many books have warned us, is actually as important as firing the gun?; or is satisfaction evolving detailed plans to outwit January cocks? There are many variations of game shooting and none are either better or worse than the others. Forget all the criticisms of driven pheasant shooting being a slaughter, which sometimes emanate from less well-endowed rough shooters, and the counter-attack that walked-up pheasants are easy targets. All shooting has good and bad features; all shooting is enormous fun, and wonderfully full of interest. Provided you enjoy it that is sufficient reason to follow your preference.

But the immediate question is what form of shooting do you want to follow? If your ambitions are simply to have a rough shoot there is no problem – decide how much rent you can afford, find the ground and then commence a modest rearing programme (see Chapter 7). The most difficult problems face the man at the other extreme, so let us consider the formation of a new driven shoot which hopes to produce a good bag, both in quantity and quality.

The first fact you must accept is that forming and running a shoot is hard work, that is time-demanding not just in the season but throughout the year. Also, unless you arrange matters carefully, it carries some financial risk. If the attractions do not outweigh the disadvantages you will be better simply taking a Gun in a syndicate, paying the money, shooting on the appointed days and not worrying your head about what goes on at the other times. If, however, you enjoy creating and organising and feel you could have succeeded as a farmer, a Staff Officer, a naturalist and a psychiatrist, then go ahead. There are times, when the chicks are dying of coccidiosis or the coverts have been poached twice in three weeks, that I wonder why I persevere. And then there comes a sunny day in the late autumn with strong pheasants bursting in all directions, and after the drive the Guns, beaters and hangers-on are animated and happy and I know why I do.

The formulator and organiser of a new shoot has the opportunity to decide his own financial involvement and you should reach a decision on this before you involve others. At the extreme we have the man who decides to make a profit. It is just possible that if he owns the ground and enjoys other advantages this can be done but, under present conditions, for most people it is not and, in any event, I am not writing this book with the object of helping such ambitions. Contrary to the spirit of the times I am not against anyone making a profit but, excepting game farmers and other professionals, I do not like to see commercialism in shooting. All field sports are an escape from such pressures. The more practical possibility is for the organiser to decide that, in return for his labours, he is entitled to a free Gun and to share the costs among the other members of the syndicate. It is true that if he were paid for his time and expertise a fair remuneration might well equal a Gun's contribution, but my view is that it is always better to work for the love of the game and pay your equal share. In this way there can be no discontent; no criticism that in a bad season you have not earned your free sport; and no personal doubts as to the fairness of the arrangement. From the practical side, as I will explain, you are also in a stronger position to call for help and financial support. This view should not be read as a criticism of those syndicate captains who enjoy a free, or a reduced-cost, Gun. The arrangement can undoubtedly be justified but I shoot with a freer mind if I know that my contribution, both in effort and cash, is above reproach.

This personal matter settled we can turn to the two essentials – the ground and the syndicate members. You may have the ground and wish to form the syndicate or vice versa. If you have the ground then the ambitions of the shoot must be tailored to its capacity and if you have the men then you must seek ground to fulfil their needs. Or, in other words, it is no use expecting a bag of 2,000–3,000 birds off 750 acres or taking a lease of 2,500 acres with a keeper's cottage when the syndicate members are men of modest means. All this may sound obvious but it is surprising how often men, given part of the equation necessary to create a shoot, will plunge ahead without logically working out the remainder.

Even when you have achieved a sensible balance between the size of ground, the anticipated bag and the cost you still have to look carefully at your degree of personal financial involvement. A faint heart will never form a good, large-scale shoot, but boldness needs diluting with a touch of wariness. Inflation is bearing particularly heavily on those men who traditionally shoot game and you must be careful not to be left holding a very lusty financial baby. It presents a very pretty problem in which you have to choose between the ability to get rid of undesirable syndicate members on the one hand and financial risk on the other. Let me explain. If you take the lease of the ground, probably for some years, in your name and then take in members on an annual basis you will have absolute power to get rid of an unsafe or otherwise unsatisfactory Gun, at the end of a season. However, if you accept Guns on an annual basis you must be prepared to allow them to resign annually. If, for any reason, the quality of the shoot falls or shooting becomes just too impossibly expensive you may find all, or some, of the members resign, leaving you responsible for the rent and other obligations of the lease. Conversely if, to avoid this risk, you make each member a party to the lease then it becomes very difficult to expel a member. Which line you follow will be determined by your financial position and how well you know the proposed members, but it is as well to decide your policy in advance.

For those readers still determined to press ahead after these pages of grim warnings and gloom, the next stage is to look at the basic economics of a hypothetical shoot. Let us presume we are aiming at a total bag of about 2,000 pheasants, which will be shot in the course of

Forming a New Shoot

ten days' shooting, eight of which will be intensive and two preliminary boundary days. This is going to be an expensive shoot, so it is wise to begin at the end and consider what quantity of sport the Guns will expect. (Of course, reasonable men will not judge a shoot merely on the bag but a sensible bag is a *sine qua non*.) In order to minimise the cost I think it practical to have a nine-, rather than an eight-Gun syndicate, (ten is usually rather top-heavy for the average shoot), and these men will expect to shoot, on average through the season, not less than twenty birds a day.

From these simple facts we can now evolve the form of our shoot. Twenty pheasants per Gun is 180 per day and in a ten-day season is a total bag of 1,800 – shall we say 2,000 which will allow an average per Gun/day of twenty-two. Now we enter into questions to which the answers vary widely according to the part of the country involved – what is simple in East Anglia is nearly impossible in Wales. I can but postulate an average and you must adjust for circumstances. To shoot 2,000 pheasants you must probably rear 4,000. I base this on a national average of 36 per cent pheasants recovered of birds reared and assume the balance will be made up of wild stock. In some areas the return will be higher and in others far lower. Pheasants follow the unjust financial maxim of, 'To him that hath shall be given', for if your area is good game ground you will not only enjoy a useful wild population but your neighbours will probably rear large numbers, many of which will stray on to your ground. To rear and hold 4,000 pheasants plus a wild population will call for not less than 2,000 acres.

With difficulty this task can be managed by a single keeper. Half a century ago it would have been impossible, but modern methods of rearing have dramatically decreased the labour factor in producing large numbers of pheasants. Even so I write, 'with difficulty', for a single man cannot carry out all the myriad tasks of a keeper efficiently. It is, unfortunately, a question of planned inefficiency, for the employment of a second man will not so change the situation that the income of the shoot can be increased to cover his wages.

Let us turn the facts into money. Immediately I face the problem that, as mentioned in the Introduction, whatever figures I give now will be out of date even before this book is published. However, there is no easy solution and readers should have no difficulty in substituting up-to-date figures for mine, for the basic needs of a shoot will not change.

Shooting rents, in 1975, were in the order of £1 an acre – rather more in the prime game counties and well under in poor ones. Say £2,000 in rent. Deducting sporting rates is a nightmare. For years they have been very low but the revisions of the last two years have brought large increases in some areas. Alternatively where the landowner becomes a syndicate member, or some parallel arrangement can be agreed, there may be no rates payable. £500 is no more than an intelligent guess. The keeper will expect a reasonable cottage but it is likely that this will go with the ground – if it does not then £1 an acre is probably too high. Additionally he will expect a vehicle. Providing this, together with his wages, National Health Insurance and other oddments will not cost less than £3,000 per annum.

The cost of the pheasants will vary according to the method used to produce them. The cheapest will be rearing from eggs, laid by birds caught up on the ground, and the most expensive buying seven-week poults from a game farm. Four thousand, by the latter method, would cost at least £4,000, but it can be argued that the keeper could then do a keeper's job and assist the wild birds to breed prolifically, rather than be a form of poultry farmer. Assuming the cheaper method, by seven weeks the shoot-reared poults would not have cost less than 75p each (this excludes, of course, the keeper's labour), which means a further £3,000.

Beaters were £4·50 per day last season and will certainly want £5 next. Assuming fifteen beaters a day at £5 each this is £75, and for ten days £750.

So far the total is £9,250. The most expensive item not yet accounted for is corn but this is not easy to price. There will be many other small items, such as wire netting and cartridges, and it will not by any means be pessimistic to round the total up to £11,000. Dividing this between nine Guns means £1,222 each, say £1,220.

It is highly unlikely that there is a shoot in the country whose costs accurately match those of my hypothetical shoot, for there are so many possible variations due to personal circumstances or local factors. However, the example serves the purpose of showing both the essential structure of a driven shoot and some idea of average costs. Your task is to consider how you can best modify the structure to suit your own syndicate's ambitions and financial strength.

Of course the number of men able to afford a Gun at over £1,000 per annum is limited, and as costs rise so shoots lose members and face increasing financial problems – a fact which has helped prompt me to write this book. In passing, I would not like to give the impression to the lay reader that the bulk of game shooting in this country is carried out by syndicates where the members all make a heavy financial contribution. Certainly the proportion of shooting conducted on these lines had grown considerably by the sixties, but the majority was done by sportsmen participating in a multiplicity of different ways and usually at considerably less expense than members of syndicates who normally have no special advantages. There are many private shoots in the farming community where the hosts, having to pay no rent, and enjoying many other facilities which dramatically cut the cost, are able to entertain their friends to excellent shooting at relatively little expense. In turn they will receive return invitations and keen shooting farmers will spend much time in the winter months shooting. I am envious but not jealous, if you take the distinction.

Some private shoot owners will recover a part of their costs by taking in a few permanent Guns and these sometimes give excellent value for money. Other sportsmen who are fortunate enough to have farming friends will receive shooting invitations and I owe a great personal debt to several very kind friends. Those readers who are not farmers will share my embarrassment at being so rarely in a position to give return hospitality.

However, I digress from the problems of forming a new shoot. The question is how to reduce costs yet still retain worthwhile sport. Unfortunately it is very difficult to reduce costs by small, measured degrees until attaining the level that suits you, for certain overheads are constant and you must either make modest changes which have little effect or sweeping ones, which alter the whole character of the shoot. Let me explain. The key to the whole situation is the keeper, for without a full-time man the whole concept of the shoot must change. You can neither reduce his wages nor dispense with his vehicle. Given this situation where the overheads of man and vehicle are rigid it is foolish to try to economise by rearing fewer pheasants, for the saving this achieves, viewed as a percentage of the total cost, is small and the sport the Guns will have will be diminished by much more than the saving warrants.

There is a case, at first thought totally illogical but I explain it later on, for reducing the cost per Gun by rearing more, rather than fewer, pheasants. This apart, the only realistic way to economise is to plan carefully a balanced scaling down all round. Labour costs have to be reduced by employing a part-time keeper, which means fewer birds reared and these require less ground. The cost drops and so does the bag – it is all a question of scale.

Economising further we reach the stage at which no keeper is employed at all and the syndicate members carry out all the work of the shoot themselves. For many men this deep involvement in the many and varied aspects of running a shoot throughout the whole year is extremely satisfying. It is certainly a more wholesome form of participation in every way than simply writing out a sizeable cheque in the summer, and later arriving on shoot days, slaying pheasants and departing. This should not be read as the conventional criticism of high-powered syndicate members. Many of them would like to become more involved but have no time. (Partly, no doubt, because they are busy earning the money to pay for their Guns!) However, whatever the reason it is better for the man and the sport if he is an active participant at all times.

Economic pressures are likely to lead to a great increase in the numbers of 'self-help shoots', and certainly the task of planning the financial aspects of their operation is much less complicated than more formal shoots. One enjoys much greater flexibility, for it is possible to take a reasonable area of ground and just experiment. With no substantial annual running costs to find the individual costs are much less and there is far less pressure to provide specific bag levels.

In the chapter with the self-explanatory title 'On a Lesser Scale', I deal at much greater length with the various ways of reducing shooting costs, but there are several other matters of common interest to shoots of every size.

One is insurance. If you are considering forming a shoot the probability is that you will know more about the sport than most of the members. Even if you do not the initiative was yours and a moral responsibility rests on you to consider the interests of everyone. It is unarguable that all shooting men should be insured against third-party claims; not so much to protect them as to prevent some poor devil maimed for life, or, worse, a fellow sportsman's widow, discovering that the culprit has no means with which to compensate. Nearly all shooting men acclaim the wisdom of insurance, but, regrettably, some never get round to arranging cover and others do but let the policy lapse after a few years. As the organiser, do not give them the chance. Insure not just the syndicate members but anyone lawfully shooting on the ground. This covers the occasional guest, boys at cock shoots, beaters on pigeon shoots and any other unexpected situation. The premium will be small and is simply added to the overall cost and shared. This action neither removes your responsibility to command safe shooting nor makes an accident less disastrous, but you will at least have a clear conscience if the worst happens.

When Value Added Tax was first announced the members of my firm were most impressed with the knowledge I displayed of its complex provisions. They were unaware that this derived from research carried out as the basis for an article in *The Field* on the effect of VAT on field sports. In practice the operation of the tax by shoot organisers is usually automatic, but it is desirable to know where it bites and how. VAT, you will doubtless know, is charged on goods or services and is borne by the ultimate consumer, unless he is operating as a business and can claim it back as an input. Unfortunately, although most forms of property were exempt there were four classes which came within the net and the grant of rights to take game or fish was one. Sporting rents, therefore, bear VAT at whatever the current rate may be. Many other items purchased by the shoot will bear VAT, from a box of cartridges to the petrol in the keeper's vehicle. The keener business brains will therefore consider whether it is not beneficial to run the shoot as a business, which would make only a minimal profit, and claim all the VAT paid out back as a business input. Alas, there is a snag. If you claim VAT back on your inputs you must charge it on your outputs – and outputs in this case would be the subscriptions paid by the Guns. (Remember VAT is payable on goods and *services* and in this case the shooting made available to the Guns constitutes a service.) As almost all the income, with a small exception I will detail shortly, to a shoot comes from subscriptions, then virtually all the income or outputs, would bear VAT, so inevitably the money recovered in VAT would be less than that paid and the shoot would be worse off. (The items purchased which would not bear VAT are quite extensive. For example, there is no VAT on labour so the keeper's wages would be VAT free. Nor is there VAT on fuel, and propane gas for brooder houses escapes. So do fertile pheasant eggs.)

A question which might trouble a new shoot organiser is whether, as the shoot is offering a service, he *must* charge VAT. The answer I formed at the time of my original inquiry, and which seems to have been confirmed in practice, is that where the syndicate members are simply joining together to share the cost of mutually enjoyed sport there is no business motive and no question of VAT arises. But whenever the owner, or organiser, sets out to make a profit a service is being provided and VAT must be charged. This explains why you have to pay VAT if you take a few days' driven grouse shooting at a sporting hotel or a rod on a trout lake. (The position is slightly more complicated in that VAT does not have to be charged when the turnover of the business is less than £5,000, but most enterprises concerned with field sports are above this level.)

No VAT need be charged on the sale of surplus game whether the shoot is profit-making or not, for food for human consumption is exempt.

2

The Ground

Having considered at length the scope of the proposed shoot the approximate area of ground needed will be known. It is no exaggeration to say that the success or failure of a shoot is dependent upon the ground. Bad keepers and unsafe shots can be removed in a few months, but it takes years to achieve fundamental improvements in poor ground. Sometimes it is impossible within realistic costs.

Although it is customary to speak of finding ground, what we, apart from a fortunate few, actually seek is the sporting rights. This process falls into several logical steps: discovering shooting rights on offer; assessing the ground and negotiating a rent; settling the lease; and, later, considering what improvements, if any, can be made.

Few shooting books give full weight to the problem of acquiring suitable ground and tend to treat the question in one of two ways. The first is to ignore the question entirely except to imply that the writer has always had ready access to, or owned, unlimited acres and presumes the reader does too. The second usually devotes a full chapter to a lengthy list of all the important essentials, with the implication that if the ground under examination falls short you should turn it down and consider the next proposal on the list. I have one such by me as I write and it is a mine of information commencing by suggesting that 3,000–4,000 acres will make a shoot of 'moderate size'! Neither approach states the reality of the situation which is that for most people it is not a question of making a choice but of searching long and hard to find a shoot and then accepting it, warts and all. A personal experience of some years ago typifies the problem. The *Shooting Times* carried an advertisement for a 300 acre freshwater marsh on the Isle of Sheppey. I wrote at once and had a telephone call from the owner who told, not asked, me to come down the next morning. Knowing my place I did and was shown round. It was August and the marsh was covered with contentedly grazing cattle. It was, I mildly observed, difficult to judge the winter duck population. 'Oh, they're there all right,' he said, 'but you must chance it – I've had seventy-three other replies.' I chanced it and all was well but the case illustrates the tremendous pressure for shooting. This obviously lessens as the level of rent climbs and, for this reason alone, your chances of finding good ground increase if you form a syndicate rather than seek a smaller area for yourself or just two or three Guns. The position has improved somewhat recently as inflation has increased the volume of shooting rights entering the market. Unfortunately some of this is land with problems where increased costs have been the last straw.

The first step is the hardest, i.e., discovering shooting rights on offer. Sometimes this is easily achieved by watching the classified advertisement columns of *The Field* and the *Shooting Times*. The drawback is that when a commodity is in short supply the owner is reluctant to spend money disposing of it by advertising when he can do so by word of mouth. Consequently those shoots which are advertised are very rarely bargains and sometimes have problems or are over-priced. (Which amounts to the same thing.) Most good ground never enters the open market but goes to a contact of the owner's who may well have had his eye on it for years. Do not be depressed – all things come to he who perseveres. Some owners prefer to let to strangers to avoid close commercial ties with acquaintances which could lead to disputes. Others want to obtain the highest possible rent and would rather conduct tough negotiations with a stranger. These owners may advertise but before doing so they will look at the 'Shoots Wanted' column and it is well worth while advertising your needs. Remember the owner wants experienced and reliable people who are going to respect his property and his way of life. Therefore do not expect the best response to a brief, penny-saving, advertisement on the lines of '2,000 acre shoot wanted. Good rent paid. Box . . .' No owner wants the embarrassment of making contact with you then having to break off because he does not like what he finds. The fuller picture he can form from the advertisement the more likely he is to emerge from hiding. If you already have your syndicate formed say so, and if it includes two surgeons, a vet and a retired Admiral give this reassuring information. Give any other facts which, if you were the owner, would encourage you to respond; for example, plans to employ a full-time keeper and rear extensively. Finally keep the advertisement running for several weeks and if it attracts no replies withdraw it for a month and try again. Obviously the latter half of the year, when some existing leases will be terminating on 1 February, is the best time, but it is worth trying at any time of the year. Many factors bring ground into the market, two of the most potent being death and bankruptcy, and the event can occur at any time.

When you do get a response act promptly. Beware of excessive enthusiasm, which will cost you dear at the negotiating stage, but view and decide quickly or you will be passed over.

As so much changes hands by word of mouth you will obviously let your needs be known among your contacts. This is effective if you know enough people in the farming community but less so if, due to having failed to get your priorities right, your friends are mainly city-dwellers. Initiative can often pay. Instead of waiting for events to occur anticipate them. If a farm is advertised for sale, attend the auction to learn the identity of the purchaser then write and ask if he wants to let the sporting rights. There are many variations.

A positive policy should be the rule – go and look for it rather than wait for it to come to you. It is well worth while preparing a list of the major estate agents covering the areas where you would like a shoot. Then write, telling them of your general requirements and, once again, give enough details to reassure. With luck your letter may arrive at an appropriate time. It could even spark off the idea of letting ground. In these days managing agents are constantly battling with rising costs and falling margins. Given an ageing client on the one hand, now unable to do justice to the shooting on all his estates, and a pleasant letter from a responsible-sounding prospective tenant on the other, the thought of splitting off some of the shooting in return for a decent rent may offer an attractive solution.

Assuming your efforts have produced an offer of suitable land the next step is assessing it. I realise that a few paragraphs earlier I suggested a prospective tenant was rarely in a position to be too critical, but a thorough inquiry into the good and bad aspects is essential, either to help in negotiating the rent or, at the worst, dropping what could be a liability. Think first in broad terms. Is it roughly the right size? If not can you sensibly adjust your own plans to fit? Is it within reasonable travelling distance or are you ignoring this in the flush of excitement? The question of how far is 'reasonable' will produce a wide range of answers. Men living in big cities must expect at least an hour's driving and often much more, but those fortunates in, say, Norwich or Salisbury, will travel far less. It is not just a question of the boredom of driving – other factors exist. One is the question of supervision, for even if there is no keeper to be visited regularly the local amateur poachers will soon discover if a shooting tenant is a distant and infrequent visitor. Money enters into the matter, for the more isolated the ground the lower the rent. Distant ground obviously has its appeal for younger men who are likely to be less affluent than their elders.

Other broad issues to investigate include the possibility of large-scale development in the area and other shortcomings also not immediately obvious. In the latter group would be a busy aerodrome which, for reasons of the wind direction on the day of the inspection, was not using the runway which sent low aircraft, at full throttle, directly over the ground. (In case this sounds far-fetched I must explain that on one shoot of my experience, lying to the west of Gatwick, the organiser has to stop issuing instructions whenever an aircraft takes off.) Among the former threats are proposals for a motorway, a sewage works, a major overhead power-line scheme, or a new town.

These points cleared, a closer look becomes possible. Always remember that even if the proposed shoot does not have all the recognised features there is no reason for turning it down if the rent takes the problems into account. For example, it may have fewer permanent woodlands than you need, but if the rent is adjusted accordingly you can afford to plant sufficient temporary cover each year.

Cover is critically important – there is little game on a barbed-wire prairie. Efficient farming deserves applause, but shooting men feel warmly towards those farmers who, whether through design or slackness, tolerate odd rough corners. Cover is either permanent or temporary, the latter coming from the farm crops which have a nasty habit of being harvested when most needed. Woods, then, are vital. It is said you cannot decide whether a mountain is climbable until you have rubbed your nose on it and you certainly cannot assess a wood from the outside. You must walk it thoroughly and decide whether it is naturally a warm, friendly wood or the reverse. Has it a good 'bottom', or is it bare trunks rising from cold soil? Ideally you want it protected from the prevailing winds by the natural lie of the ground and with a thick growth around the outside to keep out draughts. Bare conifer plantations are very poor habitat for pheasants and the ideal is a good mix of tree varieties at different ages. Finally, having said it should be protected from the prevailing winds, you need it sitting prominently on top of a hill to provide really high driven birds. It is, of course, impossible to satisfy all the requirements of ideal shooting cover but, fortunately, the pheasants will be less choosy than you and if they are warm and regularly fed will be well content.

Size and shape are important. Pheasants will not tolerate excessive densities and a small wood will never hold large numbers. Conversely extensive areas of woodland pose many shooting problems. They are difficult to beat efficiently and the pheasants quickly learn to run, unseen. Such expanses are also aesthetically unattractive to shoot, for the beauty of a wood in winter, each tree displaying its individual skeleton, is better seen from without than within. Five acres is small enough and more than fifteen acres becomes rather much. Shape can help or hinder. Narrow woods, particularly lying at right angles to the prevailing winds, are cold and square woods are difficult to beat. Given excessively large or awkwardly shaped woods the owner may be prepared to cut, or permit you to cut, suitable rides.

Apart from Forestry Commission shooting leases it is rare to be troubled by an excess of woodland – the reverse is usually the case. Quite how much cover you will need depends upon the form of shoot you plan, but all good shooting ground is a mix of warm woods and cultivated ground which, by virtue of the farming operations, provides the food the birds like. The farming operations are particularly vital for partridges, a matter I will explore in greater detail later. The ideal farm for game birds will grow plenty of cereals and not be in a hurry to plough in the stubbles. There will be kale, not fed off to the cattle until as late as possible and a variety of other attractive crops like sugar beet, mustard, maize and turnips. No matter what the pattern of the farm things will never work out perfectly. One year circumstances will take away the temporary cover sooner than you wish and the birds will concentrate in the woods, resulting in over-large bags at the beginning of the season and small ones at the end. The next year it will rain all autumn and dozens of acres of sugar beet will lie in the ground throughout November and December, holding most of your prized pheasants. (It is notoriously difficult to drive pheasants from beet and those that do flush rarely climb well.)

In the previous chapter I dealt briefly with the number of drives a shoot will need and it is important to consider whether, in this context, the ground will stand up to the pressure your plans will place on it. It will take about three weeks after a drive has been shot before the birds are using it freely once more. Assuming serious shooting does not start before early November, then each drive can only be shot a maximum of four times each season and the numbers naturally fall after each drive. Bearing this in mind, together with the number of days you plan to shoot and the number of drives you feel your team can happily manage in a day, it is simple to calculate the number of drives required and determine whether the ground provides this. If, as is highly likely, there is insufficient woodland you must establish whether the normal farming programme will provide the balance and, if so, whether you will be permitted to shoot it. If not it is essential to determine whether the owner will be prepared to grow cover crops for you and what he will charge. Agreement reached on these points *must* be incorporated in the lease for it is vital to the success of the shoot.

Water, whether rivers or lakes, and low wet areas are very welcome, for they will add interest to the shoot and variety to the quarries. For self-help syndicates and rough shooters the importance of such areas is greater.

The nearness of large towns will do more than affect the rent. Given this unfortunate blight you may be bothered by people; varying from trespassers who will picnic near nesting birds in the spring, and pick blackberries and exercise their dogs in the coverts in the autumn, to straightforward poachers. (In some ways the latter make me less angry – at least they know what they are doing.) Couples will court in your treasured quiet spots; earnest elderly ladies will seek fungi in the woods and small boys will be present in profusion. If fate is really against you there will be a public footpath straight through the heart of the shoot. It will be hell.

Consider next why the ground is in the market. You may know there is a good reason, but if not, probe. Look at the bag records – were they declining? Why? Ask if you may telephone the previous tenant for a chat. (An evasive reply should strengthen your wish.) A fall-off in results may not necessarily be the fault of the ground, but if the syndicate was to blame the owner will tell you quickly enough. Even if the results have been consistently good, look forward for possible trouble. Is extensive tree-felling due in the main coverts? And does the man who you will rent from farm the ground? If so he will want to please the shoot, but a tenant farmer, sandwiched between landlord and shooting tenants, can be most unco-operative. If you are to rent from a farming owner inquire if he has a manager and, if so, see if you can meet him. Inevitably the interests of the manager and the shoot will meet, and sometimes clash, on many occasions in the year. If he does not impress you as a reasonable man there are probably difficulties ahead and where you have other reservations an unattractive manager may justify not proceeding.

This is a convenient time to inquire into the availability of beaters, thereby avoiding the embarrassment of setting up a driven shoot and discovering that there is no one to do the driving. The need to clear the position is much greater if you plan weekday shooting when, by definition, working men are working.

By now a clear picture should have emerged of the good and bad points of the ground. If you have nagging doubts it is better to discard the project firmly than proceed, for the final objective is pleasure not worry. However, if you are to carry on the next step is rent. It is simply not possible for me to lay down any rules of thumb on the lines of so much, per acre, per county. Every factor, for good or bad, affects the rent and when you consider the large number of aspects touched on in this chapter the extent to which individual rents can vary becomes apparent. Even then I have not mentioned the critical question of the attitude of the prospective landlord and tenant, for the degree of enthusiasm or reluctance of each towards the transaction will also affect the outcome. If the ground is valuable, and the rent involved considerable, you will be well advised to retain an experienced agent, preferably a local man with knowledge of local values, to negotiate on your behalf. He will, of course, require his fee, but at least you should finish up paying a realistic rent which leaves you in a happier position if, for any reason, you are unable to carry on, with the tenancy only part completed, and seek to assign to a fresh tenant.

If you negotiate your own terms you will rarely have the difficult problem of suggesting the rent yourself. It is not unknown for a landlord to invite a prospective tenant to name a figure but the usual practice is for him to open the bidding. Depending on the man, his figure may be a fair and firm rent on which he will not drop; an unrealistically high one on which he expects market-place haggling; or any level in between. If you have assessed your man you may be able to judge his tactics, but your reply should take into account the negotiating principle that it is never wise to tell a man he is wrong in blunt terms – your purpose is to negotiate a lease, not score a victory. The valuation of any form of property that does not yield an income can never be an exact science and depends largely upon comparison with the figures achieved by similar properties in the open market. In this sense the landlord will probably have the advantage over you, as he is more likely to know the rents realised for neighbouring land. There is, however, no reason why you should not comment that you think the suggested rent is rather high and ask whether he can justify this with details of other local rents. He is unlikely to invent statistics and must either prove his argument or climb down. (Or, more probably, say he knows of no comparable ground to his!)

Whatever the outcome it must be economically viable. In other words it must be possible to pay the landlord his demands, meet all the other expenses and still arrive at a total which the syndicate members will be willing to pay.

Agreement reached we come to the lease. Before considering the terms I would stress that for all but the most minor tenancy you will be wise to have it prepared by solicitors. A good lease, which clearly sets out the rights and obligations of both sides, will often extinguish a spark of dispute before it flames up. It is uncertainty, when both think they are right, which grows to major trouble.

The essential points a lease must cover are the extent of the ground (a map attached to the lease is essential), the rent and the term of years. This is obvious. The details are not.

As mentioned earlier you must decide whether the lease is to be taken in your name or that of the entire syndicate. If the latter the landlord's solicitors will almost certainly insist that the individual members are jointly and severally liable. This means that you could still be left responsible but only if all the other members become bankrupt. I can only hope that your choice of friends makes this eventuality remote. If you are tempted to take the lease in your own name, thereby gaining greater control but also taking a greater financial risk, do remember that the lease may be for some years and circumstances may change dramatically. In the spring of 1973 I was very tempted to take the lease of 2,500 acres of ground which entered

1. Keeper, beaters and dogs at lunch on a Cumberland moor. The actual shooting days on a grouse moor are very labour-intensive and the cost absorbs some of the saving resulting from not having to rear.

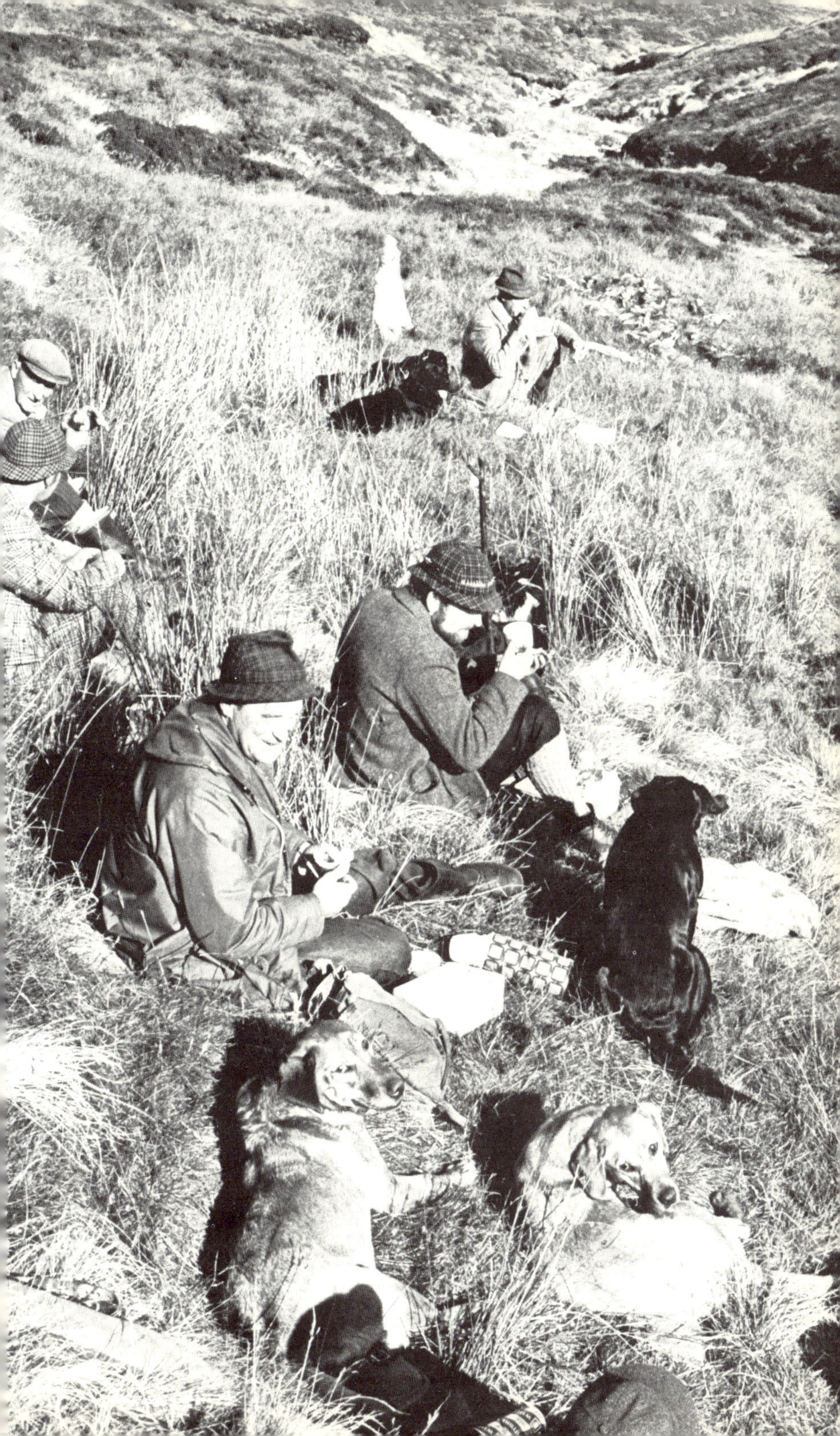

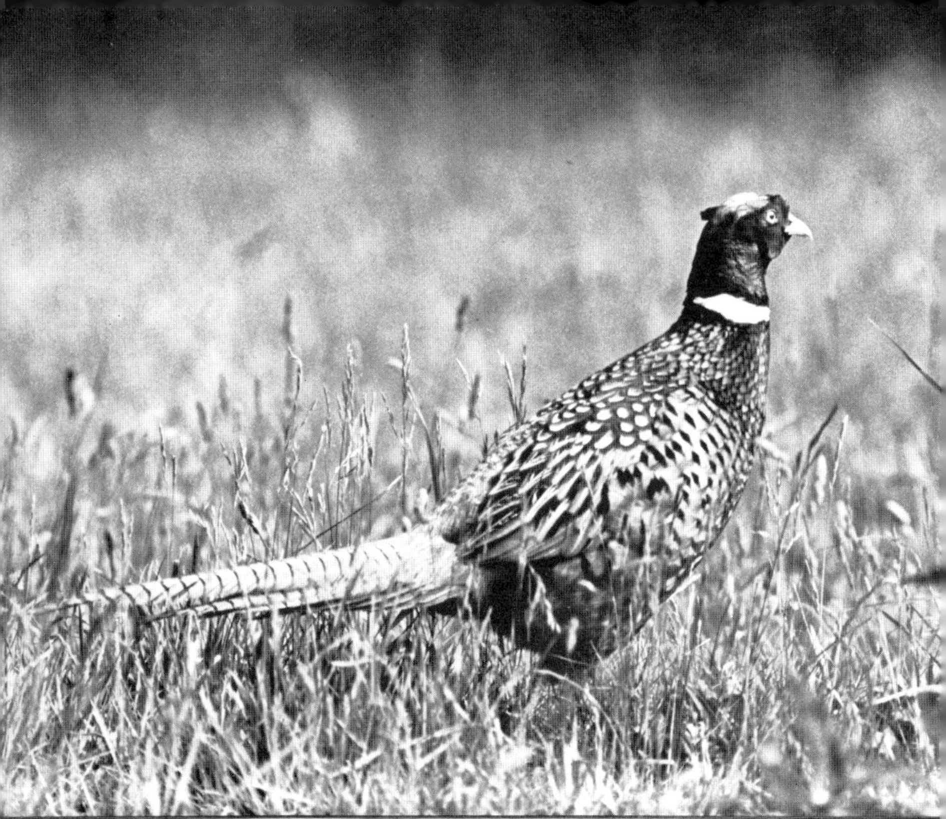

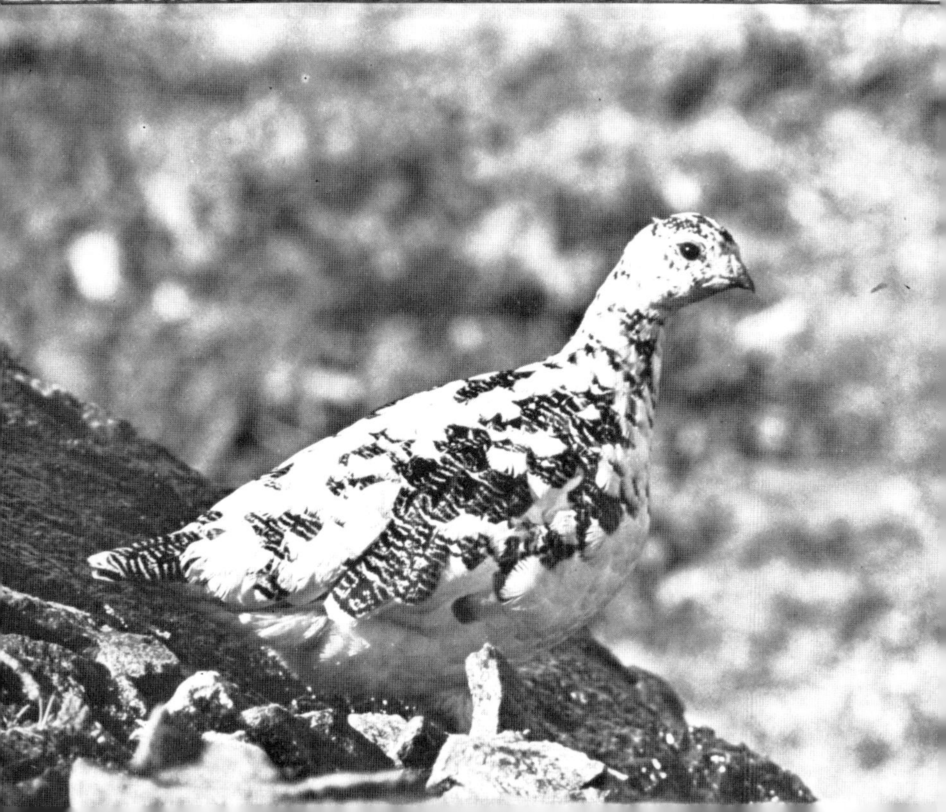

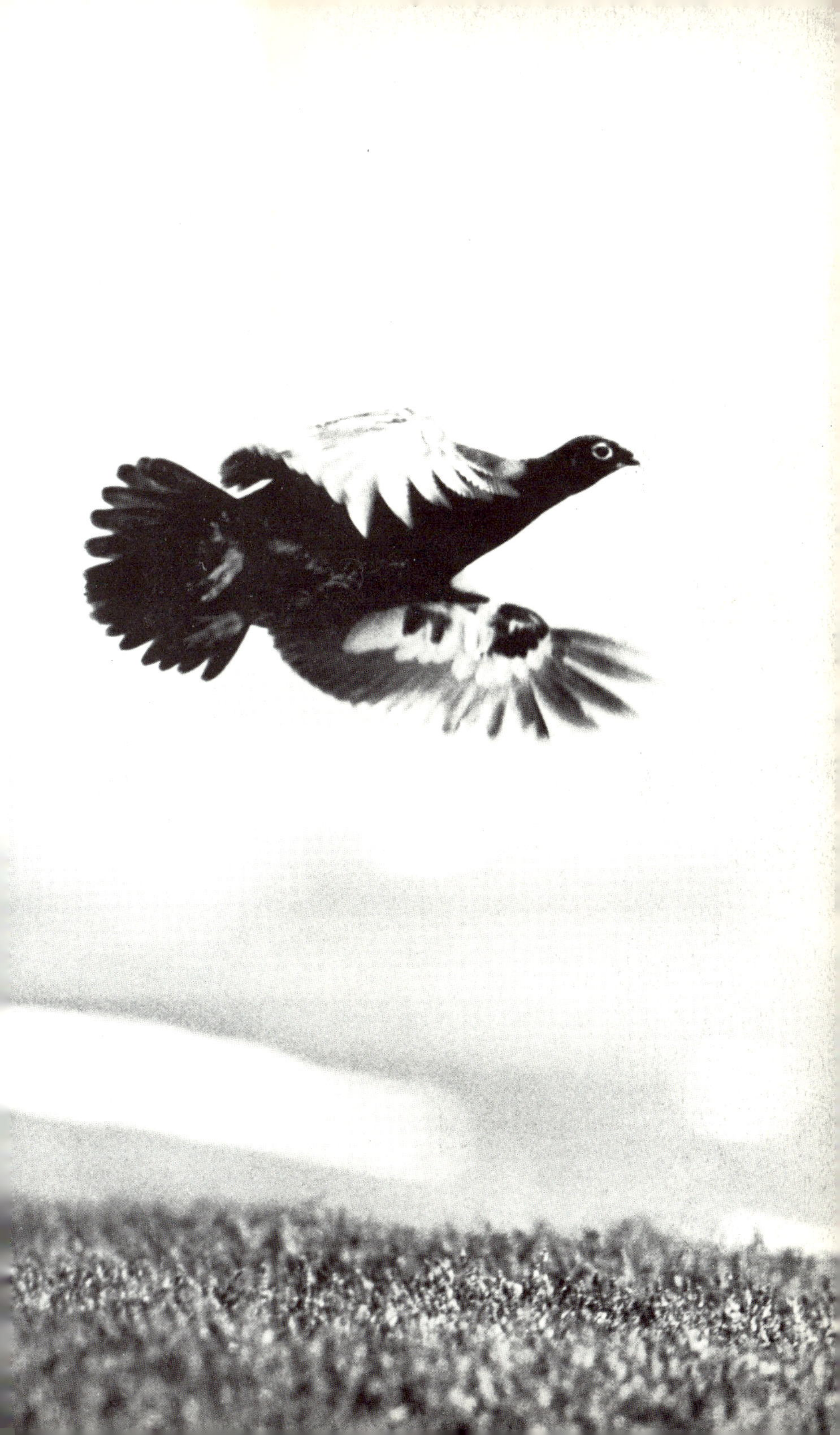

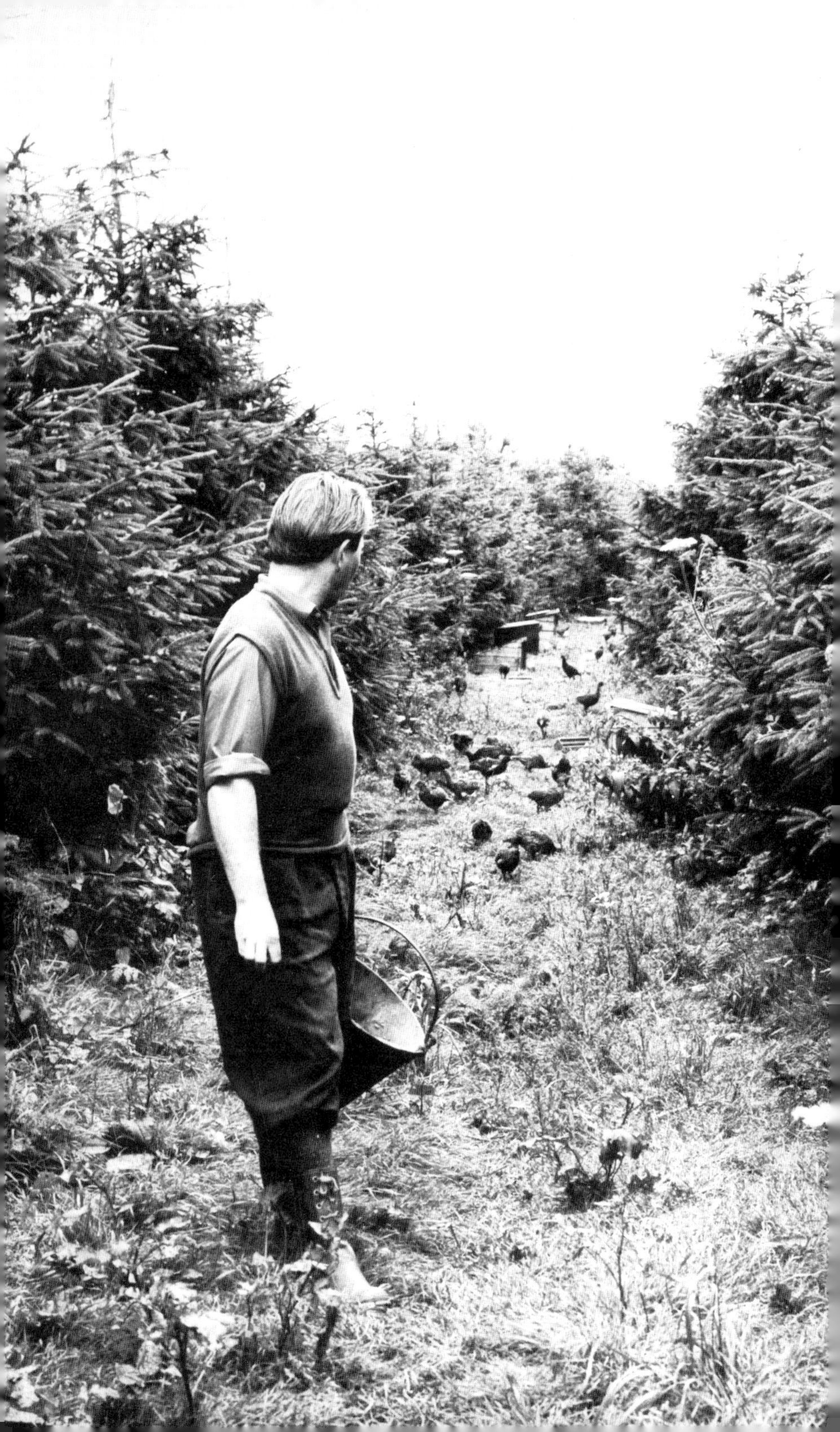

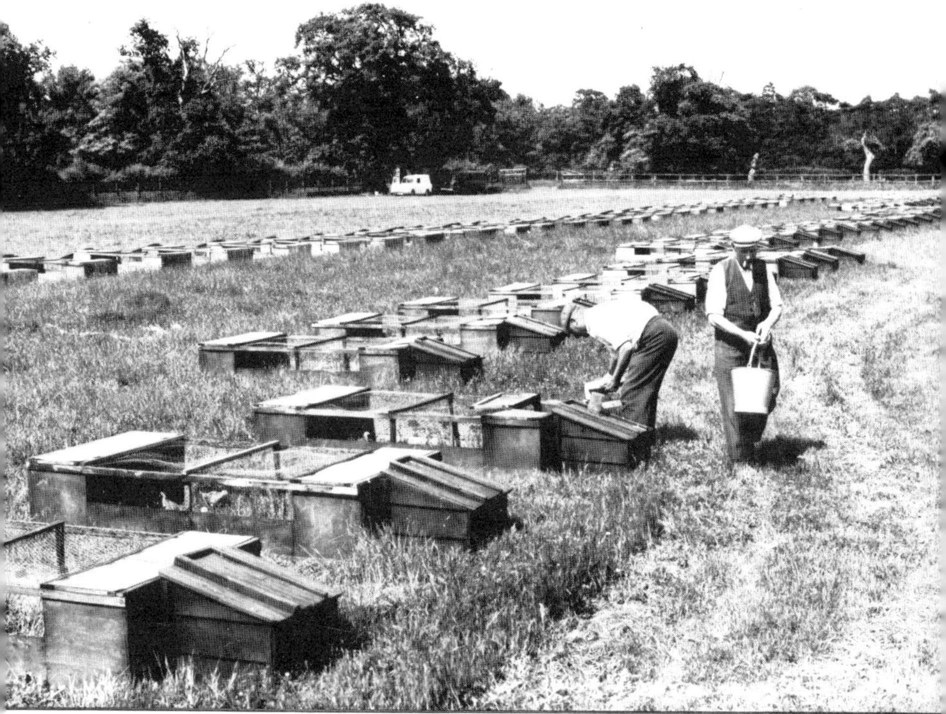

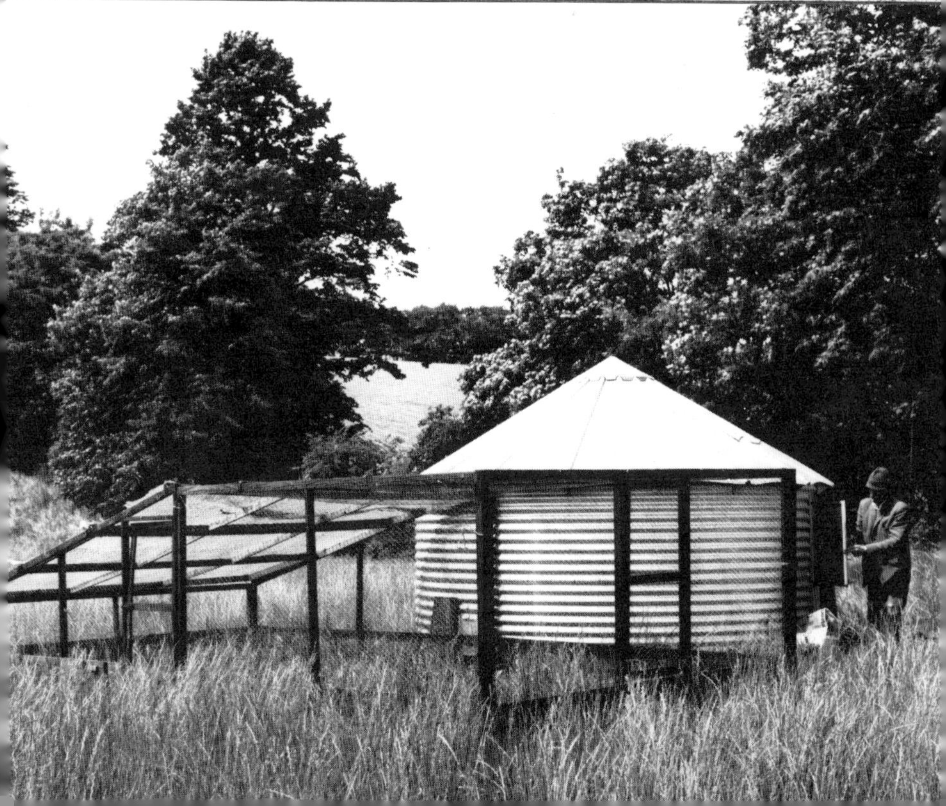

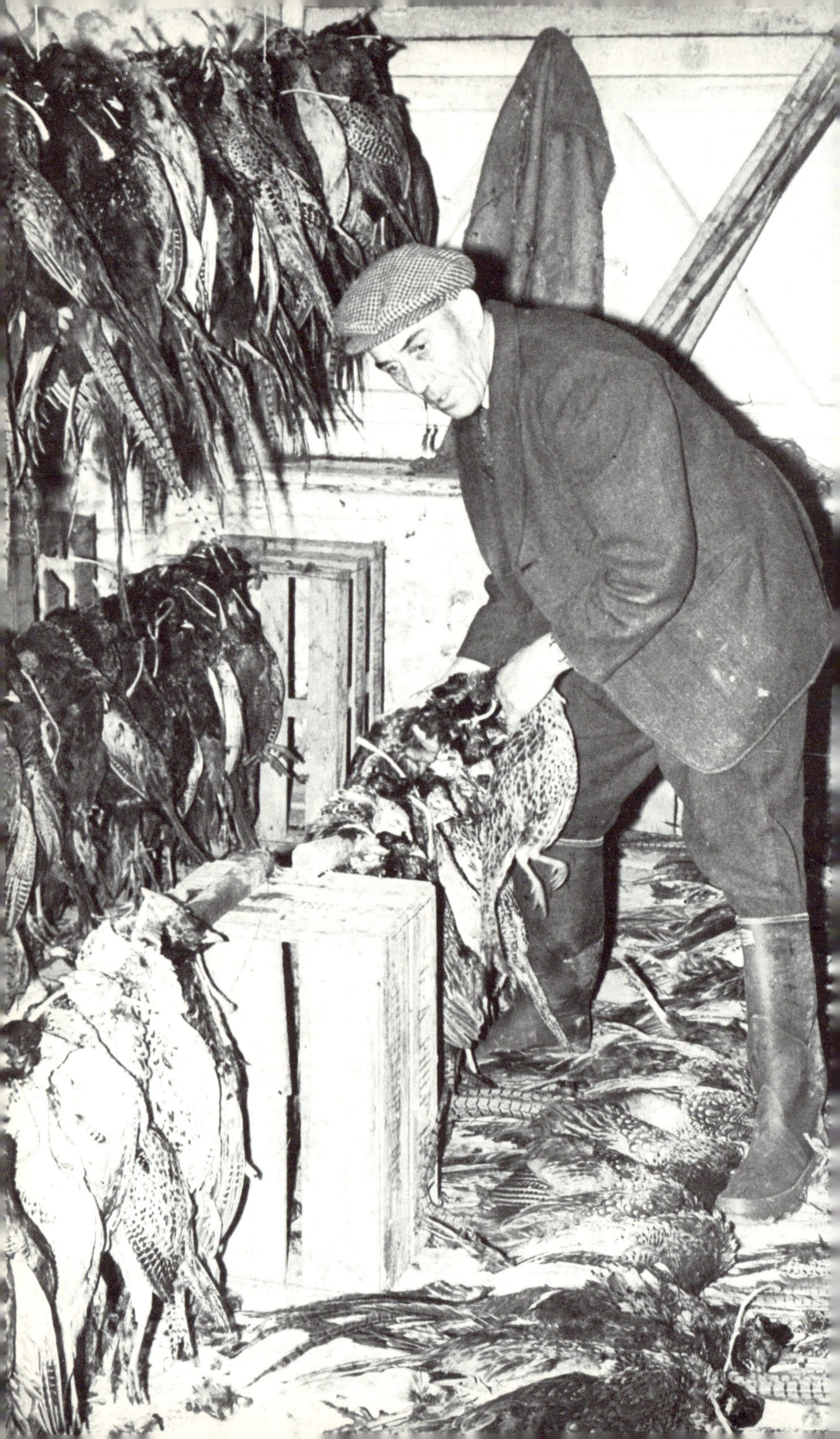

the market in mid-Sussex. Costing it out I concluded that the subscription per Gun would be rather high and that the risk outweighed the likely pleasure. Not many months later came the oil crisis and had I held the lease personally I could well have found myself with the obligation to find a large annual rent and very few men able to afford a Gun. (The man who did lease the ground went bankrupt. This was due to business problems and not the shoot but the implication was that he was a gambler by nature.)

My advice is that, unless you are in a happier financial position than most, or the shoot is a modest one, it is wiser to involve all your companions in the lease.

If possible try to have a clause inserted giving the tenants the right to assign. Then, if for any reason you find it difficult to continue, you can seek a fresh tenant rather than be forced to pay rent for rights you are not able to use. The clause in question will usually say that 'the landlord's consent in writing must be obtained', to which you should insist on adding, 'such consent not to be unreasonably withheld'. If the lease includes the use of a keeper's cottage make sure that the obligations of maintenance are spelt out, e.g. that the landlord maintains the exterior and the shoot the interior.

If the ground is good, or appears to have good potential, seek a long lease, five years at least and preferably seven. It will take three years to work things up and it is foolish to create a situation where all is going well just at the time the lease has to be renewed. This is particularly so with a run-down shoot, for if you put time and money into improving it you should be entitled to enjoy the results and not be compelled to pay a much-increased rent for your own achievements. If you lease ground where you have reservations about the potential, then it is a good idea to write a break clause into the lease giving you the power to quit at the end of the first year only. There are other clauses you should invoke for your protection. If, as is almost certain, you are going to need space for rearing birds have the lease spell this out as to where and how much. Also incorporate a restriction against forestry work in the coverts in the nesting and shooting season. (If you miss this it could be disastrous.) I call to mind the story of a friend who had the unhappy task of selling off the family farm after the death of his father. This he achieved by subdividing into several areas and, being a sensible chap, he reserved the shooting rights for seven years over a productive patch of fifty acres, composed of three small woods and a jigsaw of small fields with thick hedges. A couple of months after the sale, the new owners bulldozed everything and left a couple of vast fields with a thin perimeter hedge. One must look ahead.

Having ensured that the landlord will not harm the permanent

8. It is essential to sell game at the best possible prices, even if this creates more work.

coverts make sure that your sporting rights extend not only to these but temporary cover. If you lease sporting rights over ground the implication is that you can shoot everywhere within reason, but to avoid ambiguity it is as well to have the lease spell out your right to enter suitable standing crops, such as kale. (In case you are puzzled by references to 'cover' and 'coverts', I would explain that coverts are permanent woodlands, often planted with shooting in mind, and cover is the remainder, including crops and rough areas.)

In the later chapter, 'On a Lesser Scale', I deal with reciprocal leases where the landlord either shoots as well or retains the right to provide one or more of the Guns. This is an excellent arrangement, not least because if he is also the farmer it immediately ensures his full support for the shoot's success, but it greatly complicates the job of drafting the lease. In practice this is not so critical because the involvement of your landlord and his friends in the affairs of the shoot converts a strictly business arrangement into a personal one and a comprehensive lease has no more effect on the success of the arrangement than the words of a wedding ceremony on the future of a marriage.

On the landlord's side the lease must be expected to place various obligations on you besides that of paying the rent. In addition to such obvious requirements as respecting his fences and stock you may be obliged to employ a full-time keeper and rear a minimum number of birds each year. Whether such obligations are reasonable depends on the circumstances, but be sure to cost your obligations carefully before signing. By law the landlord retains the right to kill ground game and he is also entitled, in theory at least, to seek compensation from the shoot for the damage done to crops by game. The law on this is somewhat complex and a landlord's position is rather weak unless he can show that the density of gamebirds is well above the natural level. Obviously a landlord who had insisted on a lease requiring the tenant to rear large numbers of birds would be in a weak position if he later sought compensation for damage. A further clause in the landlord's favour, and a most reasonable one, may be a restriction against the numbers of birds shot in the last year of the tenancy.

In the end you, and preferably your colleagues, will be the proud possessors of shooting rights for a term of years. This is the time to plan your management policy, paying particular regard to how much money you have available and where it is best spent. In the following chapters I give my own views on many aspects of shoot organisation, whether large or small, but all ground needs an individual appraisal. It is rarely that there are not some simple measures that can be taken, often at little cost, which will improve sport. It may be some judicious felling in covert centres to let in light and encourage ground growth (through the fallen timber), or cutting gaps in hedges to cut off future escape routes for leg-conscious pheasants. Flushing points may need planting or draughty coverts screening. Whatever the improvements the beginning of a tenancy is the time to consider and implement them, but before doing so seek your landlord's approval. When in doubt *always* refer to the landlord.

A simple example will illustrate how relatively modest changes can bring great benefits. A single cock pheasant requires a 'territory' of about four acres, but as pheasants are birds of the fringes, that is they live on the fringe of good cover not in it, this has to be four acres partly in cover and partly over the adjoining open ground. Therefore, the number of cocks contained in a given area of woodland varies according to the shape – square woods hold fewer than long thin woods. If your ground holds large blocks of woodland the cock population will increase if you cut wide rides in suitable places, and as each cock has some four hens the number of nesting birds should improve substantially.

The Game Conservancy operate a most useful service under which they will arrange for one of their staff to inspect a shoot and offer his advice on the best ways of improving it. The men involved are all highly experienced and very practical countrymen, and their suggestions take account of what is financially possible for the shoot owner as well as what is ecologically desirable for the game. The Conservancy obviously makes a charge for this service (much reduced for members), but in terms of the annual cost of the shoot it is minimal. Even a very experienced shooting tenant should benefit by comparing his ideas with other experts and for the first-time tenant such advice is invaluable.

Improvements which involve either altering existing coverts, planting new ones or adding additional small cover or nesting areas in suitable positions can be regarded as capital rather than routine expenditure in that they will provide a permanent addition to the capital value of the shoot. Where they are substantial it is reasonable to explain your plans in detail to the owner and invite him either to contribute to the cost or to allow a rent rebate in compensation. The Game Conservancy's booklet (No. 15), *Forestry and Pheasants*, is a mine of information on improvements of this nature.

3

The Economics of Driven Shooting

It is a pity to have to sully one's sport with lengthy deliberations on money. Just occasionally, after a not very successful day, I may reflect wistfully on what it has cost but, in general, I think, most readers will agree with me that the less pleasure and money are considered together the better. Unfortunately the pressure of inflation gives me no choice for, apart from a relatively few favoured areas of the country, the hard truth for the larger-scale shoots is that unless all the essential and costly procedures are followed the bag will at once drop to an unrealistic level. For those readers in the process of forming a shoot this is a logical point at which to consider possible avenues of saving and for those already operating I hope a few ideas may emerge. There is, at least, the consolation that the greater the expenditure the greater the opportunities for saving.

While owner-farmers might be interested in my suggestions on communal rearing, etc., in general their costs are usually partly absorbed in the farm activities and the need for economy bears less harshly on them than syndicates, who have to face the full cost of every activity no matter how trivial.

The first stage in considering how money can be saved is to determine where it is going, and in this we are greatly helped by an investigation carried out in 1973–4 among ten syndicate shoots by the Game Conservancy. These were selected to give a good variety of shoots, keepers and ground, as witness the fact that the cost of a bird in the bag varied from the *average* of £4·66 to the lowest at £1·93. The running costs of each shoot were carefully analysed and totalled under six headings, giving the following results: keepering (to include wages, insurance, housing, etc.) 32·8 per cent; rearing 18·2 per cent; transport 15 per cent; rent and rates 12·7 per cent; covert feeding 11 per cent; other costs 10·3 per cent. I am surprised that transport cost more than the total of rent and rates, but I suspect the explanation could be that the shoots were enjoying long-term leases and paying rather less than full market rates.

The two most costly items were keepering and rearing, together comprising slightly more than half the total cost of the shoots and thereby warranting a careful search for economies.

Whether or not you can save costs on keepering depends very much on the circumstances: whether you have, or envisage having, more than one keeper on the ground forming the shoot. Given a plurality of keepers it may be possible, if unkind, to lose one full-time man and employ part-time labour at times of peak pressure. Parkinson's Law – that work expands to fill the time available for its performance – applies as much to keepering as anywhere else. I have a friend on the board of a large group of stores and under the present economic pressures, they cut staff by a dramatic 20 per cent. Nothing disastrous happened – the turnover stayed level and several millions were saved on wages. Most people are capable of working faster if the need exists and slower if it does not. However, the problems of managing several keepers will not bother the majority of readers and I will pass on to those employing a single-handed keeper.

Here the only obvious economy is to substitute the full-timer with a part-timer. This is impossible without changing the character of the shoot and I deal with this aspect in Chapter 5. Obviously economies are simple if you are prepared to accept a reduced standard of sport; the problem is to maintain it and save money. (In practice the target is not so much saving money as stopping costs rising.) Given that a full-time keeper is essential, economies can come only by making him more cost-effective – an ugly description to apply to a countryman but accurate none the less. The keeper represents a fixed cost; our job is to make him more effective. Given that the birds shown are of reasonable quality the test of the effectiveness of a keeper is the quantity of birds on the ground and how much it costs to put them there. Or, to come to the nub of the reasoning, if matters can be arranged so that there is more sport this can, as I will explain later, produce more income and reduce the net cost.

It is far easier to write about the need to employ a keeper as effectively as possible than to achieve this. Some shoot organisers may not know the answers and those that do may find it hard to convince the keeper they know best. Merely instructing him to follow new procedures will not suffice – he has to believe they are worth while. But the truth is that many keepers do need both direction and supervision; they are usually very good at what they do but often not the best people to decide what to do. In many cases they have been trained to a policy which was good for the estate in question, but which may be imperfect for the ground upon which they now operate. Your job is to decide what is right for the circumstances.

The main priority is to decide on the right 'mix' of effort between rearing and keepering to help the wild stock. In central Surrey, with little cereal growing and many foxes, normal keepering can be neglected and most of the effort put into rearing. On the same acreage in East Anglia it may well be possible to produce a better bag with no rearing but good keepering. Obviously the normal rearing costs would be absent from the East Anglian shoot, but to attempt this policy on unsuitable ground would be disastrous. The skill comes in estimating the 'mix'. Even on the best ground it is risky to rely entirely on wild birds, for bad weather in the breeding season can produce a bad year. Of course, in these unfortunate years you can always rush to buy seven-week poults, but the competition will be great and the price will respond. None the less it may be cheaper, when averaged out over the years, to pay a high price for poults in bad years than to face the cost of an annual 'insurance' of rearing.

Nowadays it is rare to find a shoot which relies mainly on encouraging wild birds. The reverse is usually the case, with great numbers being reared to the detriment of sound keeping. Perhaps inflation will swing the emphasis back from 'poultry farming' to keeping, for in the spring of 1975 the director of a game equipment farm told me that while orders for chicks had fallen, orders for traps had leapt. When natural keeping has been neglected for years in favour of rearing it may take a season or two to replan and regenerate the habitat to help wild birds. A reduction in vermin can be achieved quite quickly but it takes time to fence off odd corners from stock and take all the other steps necessary to develop small pockets of cover.

Rearing, at 18·2 per cent, was the next most expensive item and in hard times there is a great temptation to save by reducing the numbers reared. The savings on food, fuel and other basics are obvious and immediate and the justification is that, 'we will help the wild birds to make "up" '. Unless this intention is pursued vigorously and intelligently, and, equally important, the ground is suitable, the outcome of a reduced rearing programme is nearly always a reduced bag. This is a grave mistake. The ground should always carry the optimum number of pheasants and anything less is wasteful. The basic overheads of keeper, rent, rates, etc. remain constant and the difference in cost between a full pheasant population and a more modest one is very little when looked at as a percentage of the total cost of the shoot. The secret, I would stress again, is getting the maximum number of birds on the ground at the minimum cost. If achieving these high numbers costs more than the members wish to pay then the answer is not to reduce the numbers reared but to involve others in the extra sport available and thereby contrive a substantial income. There are two ways of doing this. One is to let one or more days' shooting to a team of outside Guns, preferably attending yourself to ensure all is well. For obvious reasons this practice has grown considerably in the last few years. I would suggest another approach. Form a syndicate with twelve Guns instead of the usual eight but with only eight shooting on any given day. In this way each Gun would shoot on two days out of three. The advantages are that all the Guns shooting would belong

The Economics of Driven Shooting

to the syndicate and the unpleasantness associated with having strangers treading your hallowed ground disappears. Additionally their subscriptions would be paid well in advance and the risk of a 'guest' team cancelling would go. It does not take much calculation to see that it is financially better to produce the maximum number of birds and have twelve Guns shooting eight days each, rather than rear fewer birds and have eight Guns shooting on eight days.

A further argument in favour of keeping the numbers of birds up, is that while most expenditure on the shoot has no immediate end-product extra rearing should produce extra pheasants, each of which has a market value. In fact given a good year for game prices the extra birds almost recover their rearing costs. This question of writing off basic overheads on the first birds is aptly illustrated by the fact that when the first new model of a car rolls off the production line it has cost several millions, but the half millionth, the overheads having been absorbed, only costs the odd few hundred pounds.

The extent to which you rely on wild birds should be partly influenced by your fellow Guns. If they are knowledgeable and reasonable men who can understand the advantages and the risks of the policy you will be more likely to experiment than if you feel that a poor season will see your Guns resign and leave you to start afresh. Unquestionably, reared pheasants, although more expensive, are safest. By the time they go to the coverts they have survived the vulnerable stages at which wild birds suffer *their* greatest mortalities.

Although I deal with rearing in detail in Chapter 6, this is the appropriate point to comment that large units, taking, say, 500 chicks are more economic in time than smaller ones. Many shoots have a hotchpotch of equipment of various shapes and sizes, built up over some years. Gather your will-power and throw the less efficient items out – it will pay in the end. It is also worth considering the wisdom of putting two batches of birds through the equipment in one season. (Personally I fill my brooders with day-olds in mid-May and then a second batch in the third week of June.) This halves the capital cost of the equipment, reduces the pressure on the keeper and allows him to give some attention to the wild birds. Also, by halving the numbers in any one process at any one time it reduces the losses in the event of a calamity. The disadvantage is that it extends the rearing season.

At this point I would ask you to note that neither here nor later am I giving advice on such details as how the keeper should catch up pheasants or whether the rearing field should face south. Any keeper worth employing will know more about such matters than me, and very probably you as well. Our function, as shoot managers, captains, organisers, or whatever name our companions flatter us with, is to stand back far enough to distinguish the wood from the trees and determine the basic policy. Furthermore if you attempt to lay down both policy and detail to a keeper he will regard you as interfering.

Let us now look at some possible ways of saving. The secret of economy in most commercial operations is to deal in large quantities, and in the case of a driven shoot this means bulk buying, bulk rearing, bulk transport, etc. To achieve this at the best level means co-operating with adjoining shoots and in general, the more the better. In this way, for example, it will be possible to seek competitive quotations from several specialist firms for the supply of a large quantity of rearing food. The price can be improved by having it delivered to a single, central point for collection by the individual shoots.

If you should decide not to hatch but to purchase day-old chicks the same principle of large bulk purchases will apply. In fact most keepered shoots will catch up sufficient birds at the end of each season to provide the eggs they need. (Can you not catch extra and sell the surplus eggs?) Hatching under broodie hens is now virtually extinct and incubators are now reliable and reasonably efficient in their hatching rate. Continuing the policy of bulk activity it is economic sense to establish a hatching centre in your area, sharing the cost of equipment and labour as before. Using multi-stage incubators, each taking 500 eggs a week, large numbers of chicks can be produced with relatively little labour. A keeper's wife, or some other competent person, could undertake the task as a part-time activity, leaving every keeper free for other work. Given sufficient experience the enterprise could be expanded to yield a saleable surplus and, as with reared pheasants and mass-produced motor cars, with the overheads absorbed at the beginning the profit margin on the surplus should be good.

The economies that can be achieved in rearing pheasants to poults can be thrown away if the numbers left on the ground by the time shooting starts have been unreasonably reduced. This can come about through either excessive casualties or excessive straying. Both factors are controlled by sensible measures but, particularly in the early days of a shoot, it is important to know what percentage of your reared birds you shoot and the extent and direction of their movements. This is only achieved by wing tagging or leg ringing; a simple enough business which can be done when the birds are caught up for transfer to the coverts. The information this yields will also tell you the percentage of wild birds in the bag. (This can be deceptive. The 'wild' birds may have been reared by a neighbour who does not mark them.) Most casualties to reared birds occur within a short time of their being put into the release pens; if they survive the first few weeks the danger becomes that of straying rather more than death. Releasing is so important that I deal with it in detail in Chapter 6, where I also cover the question of straying. But whatever measures you take they will not hold birds on cold, inhospitable ground and my remarks on cover in the previous chapter are worth studying once more. I repeat that it is bad economics to rear large numbers of birds without taking every reasonable measure to ensure that they are still on the ground in November. If the agricultural pattern of the farm is unattractive for game do investigate the possibilities of strategically placed game mixtures, which will offer both cover and food and also 'fatten-up' patches of cover which would otherwise be too small to provide a reasonable drive.

Transport, on the Game Conservancy survey, produced the surprising figure of 15 per cent. In theory it is not vital for a keeper to have the constant use of a vehicle and there is a danger that where they have they will spend too little time on their feet quietly poking around. However, a permanent vehicle has now become a perk of the job and without one it would probably be hard to fill a vacancy. Now that fuel costs have leapt so dramatically it is possible that the ubiquitous Land-Rover is no longer the most economic for the job. I suspect a Mini-van, or the like, purchased second-hand when it had suffered the maximum depreciation in value but still had plenty of working life left, would be much cheaper. Granted it would not cross country like a four-wheel-drive vehicle but the reduced cost of new tyres alone would console me to this shortcoming.

Although I think the figure of 12·7 per cent for rent and rates was below average there is nothing that can be done to reduce these two items on most shoots. In the event of shooting right values falling there is a theoretical case for approaching the District Valuer and seeking a reduction in the rateable value. However, such an act should be approached with extreme caution for there is an excellent chance that the shoot may be under-assessed and your initiative could have the opposite effect. The policy of approaching District Valuers as warily as you would a python in a thin paper bag has much to commend it.

Many inexperienced sportsmen regard the cost of covert feeding as a minor item, but the figure of 11 per cent puts it in perspective. Here again economies are difficult and the obvious measure of feeding less would be economic madness. Having spent so much putting the birds there they must have ample food or they will wander in search of fresh sources (sometimes found not far over the neighbouring boundary!). There are two angles of attack – cutting out waste in feeding and buying as cheaply as possible. I cover the first in Chapter 6. The second is usually impossible but any chance should be seized. It is worth keeping an eye open for a cereal-growing farmer who wants more shooting than he gets. An exchange of a few days' shooting for corn could be advantageous.

The remaining item of 'other charges' only accounted for 10·3 per cent but here there is a little scope for saving. Beaters, as I showed in the first chapter, are now becoming a significant expense and, consequently, worth examining as a possible saving. One step is to employ more youngsters, leavening them through the older men at a ratio of about two or three to one. They will be neither as thorough, disciplined nor quiet but, properly instructed and supervised, will do the job almost as well and for about half the money. There is a fair amount of nonsense talked about 'experienced' beaters. The job is a simple one and even the less intellectually gifted can grasp the essentials very quickly – the prime necessity is firm control.

The next beating economy will not improve my popularity in the shooting world. At the shoot I organise the bulk of the beating line consists of our own children, relatives, wives and any other friend or naïve acquaintance we can conscript. Many a 'hanger-on' standing coldly behind the Gun at his peg would be both warmer and more useful beating. Obviously there are occasions when this would not be politic but in the easier-going shoots it has possibilities.

The ultimate solution is a much greater use of dogs. As I mentioned earlier, beaters at the time of writing are earning £4·50 a day and everyone assumes it will be £5 next season. Even at this a man would earn £25 in a five-day week, which is very poor by current standards. It follows that either beaters have got to do the job partly for fun or their employment will become impractical. In this latter event there is no alternative but to resort to dogs, although I must say it is an expedient I find appealing. The major drawback in using dogs for beating is the problem of controlling them. A good line of human beaters, advancing at the right pace, keeping a straight line, tapping to prevent birds running back whenever a halt occurs and capable of being halted *en masse* at a single word, will not only flush the great majority of the birds but, almost as important, do so in a controlled fashion and ensure a steady flow rather than a few heavy bouquets. While such control is not impossible with dogs it is most unlikely and their use would see more irregular flushing and also less certainty of direction from birds. Dogs working thick, low cover are liable to flush birds in any direction and the absence of a line of tall humans also allows game to disperse over a wider arc. This is no bad thing on those drives where two or three of the Guns usually enjoy most of the sport but in other cases, and particularly at the back end of the season, birds could disperse to impractical extremes. The solution here would be walking Guns, some, no doubt, welcoming the chance to work their dogs. A team of, say, four handlers each working two or three dogs should be at least the equal of sixteen beaters in their ability to move game from cover and be substantially less expensive.

Carrying the reasoning a stage further it is not unrealistic to forecast that with proper liaison between the dog and shooting worlds, who are frequently one and the same anyway, the cost of beating with dogs could be very low. I have in mind that there are many amateur dog-trainers who would welcome the opportunity to work their dogs without thought of reward. Of course, care would be needed to exclude inadequately trained dogs but this is no problem for a firm organiser. To those who have always lived in a world in which beaters are working men who naturally expect to be paid, and anyone bringing a dog expects a bonus, the idea of dog-owners working themselves and their dogs for nothing may seem unrealistic. It is not. One of our modern problems is boredom, and the huge growth of leisure centres and other opportunities for spare-time activities illustrates this. Dog enthusiasts who want to work them need both ground and game and if we, the shooting community, provide this at great expense then it is reasonable to feel that the exchange is fair without paying as well. The arrangement will not flower overnight, but my expectation is that beating will be done less by men and more by well-trained dogs. It is worth looking at the possibilities in your area.

This advice applies even more to pickers-up and, in practice, several of the shoots within my experience already have unpaid pickers-up who welcome the opportunity. I hope that the beating and picking-up community will not feel that I am stealing their jobs. The wish is far from my mind, but if inflation drives wages ever higher and they insist on the full rate for the job the result is inevitable. Farm shoots, where many of the beaters are farm employees at a slack time of the year, will not suffer the same pressure, but I fear for those shoots where the beaters are often policemen, factory workers, and others using their spare time.

The question of beating costs should be borne in mind when planting new coverts and temporary cover strips. Where conditions permit the shapes should be such that they can be worked by the minimum of beaters.

Most of my proposals have concentrated on reducing outgoings, but it is worth examining the prospect of improving one of the few sources of income; that is, the sale of game. The majority of shoots are content to sell to a game-dealer and take his price, merely checking that it appears in line with other dealers. In fact, investigation with local butchers, restaurants, or other sources may well show that a considerably better price can be obtained. This is logical if, by cutting out the middle man you can obtain the elements of transport, storage, labour and other overheads, plus profit, which would have gone to him. The reasoning breaks down if the dealer can export to the Continent and obtain a substantially better price than in this country, but at the moment this is not the case.

4

The Organisation of Driven Shooting

The various functions of a driven shoot are complex and, like all complex activities involving human beings, whether or not the proceedings flow smoothly or range from muddle to outright chaos, depends largely on the man in charge. The task facing a shoot organiser has grown more formidable over the years, and particularly so for the syndicate captain or manager. The old-time shoot owner was in an extremely strong position and could speak with the authority that often went with being not only the freeholder of the ground but a leading pillar of local, and even national, society. The modern manager frequently commands on no more slender foundations than his own personality and character. (Although as he usually does a great deal of work for no reward other than personal satisfaction, the threat of resignation should make any recalcitrants think again.) The modern problem is increased by many men coming to shooting from a town background and thereby lacking the natural country background in which most shooting men of the older school grew up. Nor is the situation helped by their not being able to afford game shooting until they have achieved success in their careers and are thereby often less humble in their approach.

The manner in which different men manage their shoots varies, but let me declare myself immediately as being in favour of firm, positive control. It has been my experience in all areas of human collaboration, both in business and a wide range of social activities, that everyone involved is happier and results are better when the leader is decisive. Of course, I am not advocating a dictatorship, or a situation in which the views of all the members are not invited and weighed, but in the ultimate the leader must have the power and the character to decide what is best and put it into effect. At no time is this more important than shooting days. Occasionally one visits a shoot at which every decision is preceded by a huddle of figures, from which emerges a communal decision with which no one is completely content. Have none of it – agree the policy of the shoot when it is formed, then go boldly forward doing the job. If you avoid using your position to give yourself petty advantages, try to see everyone gets his full entitlement, and, if possible, maintain everyone, from the humblest stop to the mightiest guest Gun, in the best of humour, then you have no cause to feel uneasy. You may not get thanked but you are unlikely to be shot out of hand.

Organisation begins with the formation of the shoot members; the team, as it were, and it is no exaggeration to say that this stage determines whether the whole enterprise is to be enjoyable. Given good ground and a good keeper you can hardly fail to produce a large annual bag, but if you are to experience the glow of happy companionship that mutually shared sport brings you must pick your men with care. I would not presume to tell you how, but if after meeting a man you ask yourself the question 'Did I like him?', and cannot give an instant affirmative then you would be wise to look elsewhere. If you are to meet men and then draw back you will find it wise to follow the practice of a well-known if not universally liked politician, and keep your options open. If you advertise vacancies for Guns, then any refusal to accept an application must cause offence. Better to talk of an anticipated vacancy which can, if necessary, fail to arise.

Your position may vary from the syndicate organiser forming a complete team of paying Guns, to the private shoot owner reluctantly taking in a paying Gun or two to meet increasing cost. The latter is the trickier situation for you will now have two classes of Guns – pure guests who are grateful for your kindness and will not be too fussy over the bag, and men who have paid out cash and expect value for money. The problems worsen if any antipathy develops between the paying Guns, whose money you need, and the others whose friendship you value.

As an aside, I am not being wholly accurate when I suggest that guests will not be too bothered by the size of the bag. In many cases invitations to private shoots are reciprocal to the point where the situation becomes a form of high-class syndicate in which money is not mentioned. A typical situation will involve shoot owners A, B and C, who both give and receive invitations among themselves. Provided the level of sport remains fairly even all is well, but if A rears fewer birds and the bag drops dramatically, or even worse, forms other friendships and invites B and C less often, it will not be long before his own presence is requested less frequently, and the social geography of an area is reshaped.

The organiser of a new syndicate starts without such pressures, although if he has already signed the lease for the ground he is not a man without care. Unquestionably Guns are best found by personal recommendation, and here an extensive range of shooting friends is essential. Without this you are driven to advertising in the sporting press and this I would urge you to do under a box number. The advertisement should be fairly expansive on the details of the proposed shoot and, in particular, must be forthright on the likely cost. There is no shortage of people seeking cheap shooting and it will save time if you eliminate all who cannot match your financial plans. The advertisement should also call for some details of the applicant's shooting experience. It is a reasonable request and any evasion should invite suspicion. Behind this shield of anonymity you can then sift the replies and, in particular, look for any mutual contact with whom you can make discreet inquiries before emerging into the open.

Once you meet a potential Gun it is reasonable to discuss his shooting background, making the point that he is no doubt pleased at your insistence on safe shots. If he has recently left a syndicate I think it is perfectly permissible to ask why and to seek permission to approach the organiser. Here again a hesitation to grant permission invites suspicion. It is at these interviews that the wisdom of my advice that the shoot organiser should not enjoy any personal advantage or profit will emerge. The fact that you are doing the job for the benefit of the members, and gain no personal reward, confers a strong moral authority. Whenever possible investigate a man's shooting background – you have an obligation to the other members of the syndicate to do your best in this respect.

It is as well to lace the altruistic euphoria in which you are labouring for others for no reward with a dash of human cynicism. Or, in other words, spare some thought for protecting your own position. I do not think the law has ever been called upon to define the precise legal relationship between the individual members of a non-profit-making shoot. I hope it never will be. However, if your judgement of humanity errs it is just possible that you and your syndicate might make legal history and, this being an expensive way to fame, you should go to some trouble to avoid it. Never make promises about what the syndicate is going to do. Speak of what you plan to do, and the results which you hope will accrue, but not of definite numbers placed in release pens, or dead birds at the end of shooting days. If you are so foolish as to make these promises on paper it might be held that you, or the syndicate, had entered into a contract in which X, in return for a certain sum of money, was guaranteed certain sport. I know an actual Hampshire shoot which was attacked by a Gun on these lines, but the outcome is not helpful to us as the purpose of the shoot-owner was to make a profit.

In spite of this warning I still think it is important to evidence the arrangement in writing, and in Appendix B I suggest a possible form of letter. In this you will notice that I make it clear that the syndicate organiser carries out his function on the basis that he neither claims any special advantage nor accepts any greater responsibility than the other Guns. We return here to my earlier point that you must decide whether to take the lease in your name and thereby carry the responsibility but have the power to dismiss unsatisfactory companions, or to lose this advantage and involve your colleagues in disaster as well as success. If the latter you must make sure your companions do not fade away when trouble looms. My proposed letter states that the syndicate is a joint venture and, as such, all members assume an equal responsibility for any liability that may arise.

This may all sound very ponderous, but years of business have taught me that fate comes up with some strange situations and he who provides in advance blesses his own foresight. Consider, for example, the syndicate formed on a casual, word-of-mouth basis. Regrettably a stop, partly concealed in a ditch, is shot. The widow, who the previous week was accusing him of being an idle layabout discovers his true virtues and sues for £80,000. The guilty Gun protests his innocence on the grounds that he was unaware the stop was there and blames the organiser – you. The Judge is partly convinced and divides the damages equally between you and the Gun. You then counter-claim against the other members of the syndicate on the basis that it is a common venture. They all then retire smartly behind their various solicitors and you have as much chance of seeing a financial contribution as a young, newly entered gill ferret has of reaching the throat of an old buck rabbit snugly tucked head-on into a narrow burrow . . .

This leads us neatly into the question of insurance. Years ago I organised a small grouse moor syndicate and as our landlords reserved two Guns for their own guests we saw a great variety of visitors, culminating in the high-powered Frenchman who flew over in his private plane. In his enthusiasm to fire at almost everything, nothing under 120 yards being disregarded, he omitted accuracy, and it was only on the last drive of the last day that he actually shot a grouse. This detail, although not to be forgotten, has not impressed itself on my memory as much as seeing him advance into his butt and put on a pair of spectacles, complete with side-shields, made of plain, but armour-proof glass. This prompted me to effect the insurance I really should have arranged when the syndicate was first formed, and since then I have never omitted this precaution. It is wise to have the policy so drawn that the insurance provides cover for any accident on the ground in question rather than for named individuals. This eliminates the risk of an accident with a non-regular Gun. The cost of such insurance is relatively trivial and the relief it could one day bring enormous. It goes almost without saying that the possession of insurance cover in no way eases the need for the strictest observance of safety.

I deal with certain specialist aspects of safety in Chapter 9 but, in general, I will not dwell on it. The need for insisting on gun safety is so obvious, and the rules are so well known, that there is no point in my labouring them once more. Two points, however, are worth underlining. Firstly, if you are not very safety conscious you should not organise a shoot. Secondly, as I detail later, you have a moral obligation to everyone in the field to be extremely firm over the strict observance of safety rules.

To avoid embarrassing differences later it is important to have a clear understanding at the outset on the related questions of the payment of subscriptions and substitute Guns. The first rule on subscriptions is not to fix a definite figure, but to arrive at an estimate, preferably slightly higher than lower, and make it clear that, while any surplus will be refunded or credited to next year's subscription, any deficiency must be made up immediately by the members. This procedure avoids the obvious risk of quoting a definite figure then finding a dissatisfied member, or members, proving awkward over making up any loss. The payment of subscriptions must be so arranged that the syndicate always has money in hand but does not require the members to pay too much too soon. I suggest a fair arrangement is to halve the anticipated figure, and arrange for one payment at the beginning of February and the other at the beginning of August. Both these payments may seem early but there are good reasons. In the case of February the new shooting year has begun, and apart from rent, rates and keeper's wages, the heavy expenses of rearing must soon be faced. The August payment has a further justification than being half way through the shooting year. If any Gun is feeling half-hearted, or has hit financial problems, it is much better to find out with a reasonable period of time left in which to seek a replacement before the season begins. Even so most shooting men who are contemplating a change make it immediately a season has ended, and it will not be easy to fill a vacancy even starting in August. This minor time advantage will be lost if you are slack over subscription collections, and it is wise to send a reminder several weeks in advance and give slack payers little grace. In August you at least have the advantage that Guns have already paid a half subscription and will not want to lose it. However, if anyone wants to withdraw you are perfectly entitled to refuse to return the original payment until a replacement has been found, and then to deduct any costs involved. This may sound a rather hard attitude, but if you return the original subscription and then cannot find a replacement Gun you have either to invite the other members to join you in sharing the loss, or to sue the offender. The first alternative is unfair to your colleagues and indicates bad management on your part. The second is distasteful, costly and has no guarantee of success.

The matter of substitute Guns require careful thought, for if you do not spell out the rules in advance you will one day be faced with a tricky decision and no time to ponder the answer. The crux of the problem is this. Driven game shooting is an expensive business and if a man pays his share and then has to be unavoidably absent it is rather unfair if he is denied the opportunity to fill his place with a friend. The counter-argument is that safety standards vary so greatly nowadays that the friend may be unsafe. At the worst there can be an accident, and at the best you have the embarrassment of censoring a member's guest. There is also a danger that if substitute Guns are permitted for unavoidable absences the practice can increase. 'Unavoidable' absences become more frequent as a Gun exchanges days with a friend on another shoot, and in extreme cases a member could even sell a day or so to a 'friend'.

There is a strong theoretical obligation on you, as the organiser, to ban all substitute Guns but what is reasonable in theory is often very difficult in practice. (Like the necessary lead to hit a fast pheasant!) The best compromise, in my view, is to make it plain that no one may send a substitute Gun unless he has personally shot with him and is prepared to vouch for his safety. Merely knowing him socially as a decent fellow is not enough.

I do not think it is for you, as the organiser, to rule on this matter, particularly if you favour allowing substitute Guns. Statistically one of the other members is more likely to be shot than you are and the syndicate should be allowed its say. If the majority are against substitutes I would suggest an alternative. This is to prepare a list of men, known to be safe, who would be interested in purchasing an occasional day's shooting and who could be approached at short notice. Their payment would be handed to the absent Gun, although to make such an arrangement attractive to the spasmodic 'guests', the charge would probably have to be lower than the true figure. The loss would have to be borne by the absent Gun and would be his penalty for allowing some such trivial matter as a business crisis or a twenty-fifth wedding anniversary to interfere with sport.

There is a final alternative, which is to have the syndicate agree at the start of the season that absent Guns be filled, with no reimbursement to the absentee, with a guest of importance to the syndicate; for example, the shoot owner, the tenant farmer, the agent or, perhaps best of all, the Chief Constable for the County. In spite of my firm attitude on substitute Guns, in the event of a member suffering ill health, or some other set-back, which deprived him of most of the season's sport there is an obvious case for the syndicate doing its best to let the Gun or refund at least part of the subscription. Even if the Gun could not be let the remaining members will have shot much the same bag and, it follows, enjoyed individually more sport.

Ideally one should avoid half Guns – that is the practice of a man paying half the subscription and shooting on half the number of days – for this increases the work to the organiser and doubles the chance of finding a member who is either unsafe or does not 'fit in'. Unfortunately in these days half Guns are often unavoidable. It helps if two half Guns know one another, or you introduce them and you then arrange to deal with one only. Then in the event of a cancellation, or any other cause for contact, you do not have to search your records to see which is shooting. From their side there is the advantage that they can chop and change dates as they wish, possibly with one man shooting more and paying more, and no one minds. Avoid the temptation of confirming the membership with only one of such a pairing; the legal relationship of the syndicate is equally strong with each.

If two friends share a Gun they have the disadvantage that they never shoot together. If you have two such pairs of half Guns it is worth suggesting the pairs of friends shoot together on alternate days. Slightly complex, I appreciate, so to explain: if A and B are friends and so are C and D, A and C will normally shoot on the same day and at the following shoot so will B and D. This pleases no one, so on the first day A and B can shoot together, on the next C and D, and so on. Having gone to this trouble to please all four it will then be discovered that either the AB Gun or the CD Gun has had the better days; and the losers will lament the fact. It is details such as this which age shoot organisers prematurely.

Remember that being a shoot organiser does not oblige you to do all the work. Given a pleasant team of Guns, and if they are not the fault is probably yours, it is sensible to share out some of the work. Any accountant or banking member will, after years of being the Honorary Treasurer for everything from the Boy Scouts to the New Church Spire Fund, offer only a token resistance to the position of treasurer. If you have a slightly twisted sense of humour and a member who occupies some large post in commerce, ideally conducting international sales deals in the order of six figures, put him in charge of negotiating the sale of the bag to the local butcher. With care and planning it may be possible to assign so much of the work that you can actually commence a shooting day with a good part of your mind concentrating on personal pleasure.

One of the most vital steps in formulating a new shoot is the appointment of the keeper and, in view of its importance, I deal with this matter at length in Chapter 6.

Another step which is best done sooner than later is identifying the owners or organisers of neighbouring shoots and paying a courtesy call. An early visit shows an enthusiasm for good relations and will scotch the wild rumours that usually precede new arrivals. Invariably there are many points of mutual concern and you, as the newcomer, should learn much on such aspects as the best pickers-up and the ways of the local poachers. Assuming your keeper is new to the district it is important to see that he quickly meets and establishes a working relationship with other local keepers and the police. At this stage in the life of a shoot it is well to bear in mind that knowledgeable men will judge your efforts not just on the numbers of birds shot but their quality. In Chapter 9 I deal with some ways of making your birds fly higher and faster.

After this early season bustle of activity with your fellow Guns they are left in peace while your concentration moves to the keeper and rearing. This aspect is covered in Chapter 6, but in due time the season looms and with it the question of organisation on shooting days. It is preferable to fix the actual shooting days well in advance – months rather than weeks. Left too late you are under constant pressure from your Guns to revise and alter because your proposals clash with other dates already fixed. There is no charge for planning well in advance. Never pass dates by word of mouth; somebody will misunderstand. It is well worth writing individually to members, and if there is more than one assembly point ensure that the correct place is given alongside each date. Written confirmation of dates should also be sent to the keeper, pickers-up and, if only as an act of courtesy, the landowner or farmer. Your notifications should always include the time, and if you expect punctuality from everyone else you will be there well in advance yourself. After the first few shoots your performance will have established whether this is one of the lackadaisical shoots where everyone always seems to be waiting for a Gun, the keeper or the beaters, or a crisp, on-the-mark organisation where a Gun arriving a few minutes late feels guilty and apologises.

A good organiser will plan the day well in advance and ensure that the keeper and other key figures know the details. In practice, of course, the sequence of drives will have been settled with the keeper, often some weeks in advance, although you should not blindly follow the plans irrespective of conditions on the day. For example, if a gale springs up there is no point in attempting to drive birds into it. Either change the drive, take it the other way or place the Guns behind the beaters instead of in front. Plan the drives so that they 'feed' each other, that is the birds from one drive will be driven into the next and so on. Also, unless circumstances make it impossible drive your coverts towards the centre of your ground and not the boundary. Common sense also dictates commencing the day with the outermost drives and working in rather than the reverse.

Do not be content with merely selecting the drives. Visit each of them with the keeper and discuss the details. Decide the position of each peg and how you will adjust them if the wind plays tricks. It is very important to take account of the wind on shooting days, for if ignored it can spoil several drives, and if used it may produce the best birds of the season. The position of stops and pickers-up should be settled now, when there is time for quiet consideration, and not on the day when snap decisions are inevitable. Decide how the beaters will reach the covert, where they will enter it, and whether they will advance consistently or if a wing should hang back to edge birds in a particular direction. Having made these plans look upon them as provisional only and not a blueprint for years to come. Observe carefully what happens on the day – do the birds rise where you expect? Fly where they should or show a tendency to edge to one side or go back? Do you spy the odd bird slipping down an unstopped hedge? Or are the pickers-up too near or too far? It will take several years before you have all the details right. Nor if you have taken over both a shoot and its existing keeper should you assume that the tactics which have been followed for years are right. Naturally in all these matters you will consult with the keeper rather than instruct. If he finishes the day with the belief that all the good ideas were his then so much the better.

Reverting to stops – they provide a good example of the need for flexibility. On cold, grey days the function of a stop is to prevent birds slipping out of the covert without taking wing when the drive begins. As such it is sufficient for him to be in position only a few minutes before the arrival of the beaters. But on a sunny day, and with attractive fields near by, he has to take his station much earlier to keep birds in which would otherwise wander for natural reasons.

Like all shooting men you will have suffered from days when no matter which peg you occupy the birds fly elsewhere. There are even bad spells when this goes on for several successive shoots. With this in mind you may be tempted to try placing the Guns yourself, rather than having them draw for positions to ensure that each gets a fair share of the shooting. Don't! You will fail miserably. In a short time one Gun will have shot many and another none. Try as you will throughout the day the gap between them will widen, the sufferer will hate you, the lucky one feel guilty and your own day be ruined. Draw and let fortune bestow her favour – over the season it will average out. (Although I write this, I have a nasty feeling that it is not true. I have a Hampshire farming friend who seems to act as a magnet to game. There are other men who are nearly always unlucky. One can only tell them the experience benefits their character.)

Although it is wisest to let Guns take their chance from the draw, this is not to say you should not help fortune to average out her

The Organisation of Driven Shooting

blessings. The need to use each drive to 'feed' the next means that drives are normally shot in a set sequence. Studying the results obtained from drawing each number will show they frequently do not average out in the course of the day and one number will always give more sport than another. To explain: let us suppose that number 4 on the first drive is good and the Gun still has a good position on moving to number 6 in the second drive. In the third drive at number 8 the birds might always tend to go back and give him plenty of chances, and on the fourth drive at which he will be number 2, the prevailing wind might favour low numbers. This combination of luck might endure with all his numbers throughout the day. Conversely another Gun could draw a number which is consistently poor, including that double blow fate occasionally deals when you find that on the two drives upon which you occupy a centre position you face the poorest coverts on the shoot. A good organiser will note these sequences and produce a series of cards in which the Guns' positions do not just move up by two after each drive but are balanced to attempt to give everyone a fair share of the sport. I first experienced this practice on a famous Cumberland grouse moor, and it was fascinating to see how the individual drives gradually balanced out the sport to all the Guns. Another advantage of the system is that Guns change their neighbours throughout the day, which makes for greater variety and fellowship.

You will be aware of the need to start the season with outside days, but have perhaps never considered all the reasons. These days are almost a form of training exercise for all concerned. The Guns can regain their form; dogs can be steadied; new beaters assessed; and all the procedure of the shoot sharpened up. Not only are birds straying dangerously near the boundary bagged, but the disturbance around the perimeter pushes the others back towards home. And those birds which escape will in future be warier and fly better. From your point of view the Guns, starved of sport through the last eight months, will not be too demanding, and you can please them without losing too many birds. All in all these outside days are very useful.

This question of bag adjustment must occupy your mind. The ideal is to shoot a modest but sufficient bag in the first few days, and then to rise to a sensible bag which is maintained at the same level throughout the season. The opposite extreme is to kill large bags in the first few shoots, when the birds are poor flyers, and leave little stock on the ground for the later shoots. It is not difficult to achieve the right levels if you plan sensibly and remain flexible. Few shoots have coverts of constant quality, and the 'mix' of drives can be selected to give the bag result required. Common sense requires you to spread the good and the mediocre drives throughout the day to prevent boredom, although it is psychologically sound to make the last drive of both the morning and the afternoon good ones. Do not hesitate to vary the action on the ground to produce the result you want. If a covert is likely to hold more birds than you want over the Guns, then put the beaters in half-way through. This is the time when your previous close liaison with the keeper will bear fruit. For example, if a covert holds many more birds than you both expected, and an unwanted slaughter appears imminent, he will quietly rearrange his beating line and allow an escape route. Always remember that you can only kill a pheasant once.

In planning drives bear in mind that once a covert is shot it will take some two to three weeks before the survivors are back, and every time you go through you make a further reduction in the population which cannot be regained except at the expense of your other coverts. (In theory you can attract birds from neighbouring ground, but in practice you probably lose as many as you gain.) The mark of a really good shoot organiser is his ability to balance the bag throughout the season. Of course, you cannot expect to shoot as many birds in January, with many hundreds already bagged, as you did in November, but the contrast should not be over-dramatic.

When you start shooting is partly dictated by local conditions but, as I explain later on the subject of quality, I am a strong believer in starting the season late and finishing late. Certainly I would discourage shooting pheasants before the last week in October.

You will perhaps have noted that after all these words the actual day's shooting has not yet started. This is deliberate, for the more planning done in advance the smoother the day will go.

One matter which needs settling well ahead is your attitude to ladies – do you or don't you want them at a shoot. This may sound very Victorian, but some men object strongly to having ladies at a shoot and others welcome them. It is for you to test the wind and make the position clear. Personally I welcome ladies in the belief that the purpose of shooting is not to kill things but to enjoy a day in the country with good friends and good spirit. Continuing this reasoning a stage further, if you agree then let this philosophy pervade the day. If a man is shooting badly then do not fuss about missed birds, but thank him cheerfully and comment that if everyone would do the same the shoot could have another couple of big days. Equally, if the keeper misunderstands and a drive goes wrong, then what of it. A few pheasants lost is a minor irritation and they are left for next time. You, as the leader, set the tone in these matters, and merry laughter in a shoot is worth a lot of pheasants in the bag.

Before the day begins make sure all the Guns, and particularly any guests or substitutes, know what is expected of them. I deal later with the tricky question of foxes, but leave Guns in no doubt as to whether they are to be shot or not. Make sure they know whether the shoot numbers from the right or left, and the signals you use to start and finish a drive. If you prefer, as I do, to see guns broken whenever men stand together then say so. If it is later than Christmas leave them in no doubt whether hen pheasants can be shot. Finally deal with the question of the extent to which Guns should use their own dogs on difficult runners, or whether time requires these to be left to a picker-up. If the latter the Guns should know how to get a message through, as a properly placed picker-up will not be close.

Avoid *all* communication by shouting – nothing causes game to depart as much as the human voice. Use whistles, horns, flags, or what you will, but at all costs keep everyone quiet. Have no hesitation in descending politely and firmly on any offender (of either sex), for once the rot sets in the shoot will sound like a cocktail party.

Even now we are not quite ready. The beaters' wages should be on hand for the finish and it is wise to have a first-aid kit available and also spare cartridges. (You will have noticed it is always the same men who run short.)

Sport can now begin.

Lunch arrangements often present problems for the organiser and, all too often, are determined by the ages of the Guns and their love of creature comforts rather than the interests of the shoot. While I readily agree that the enjoyment of the participants is the main objective the needs of the pheasants must take priority. It is most important to finish shooting for the day when there is still enough daylight left for the birds which have been disturbed to return to familiar territory before they settle for the night. With this in mind I prefer to keep lunch fairly short and am quite content with a snack in a barn. This practice also facilitates getting the party on their feet afterwards, an advantage that will be appreciated by anyone who has tried to separate a group of Guns from an open pub fire on a cold, wet day. If your members are content with a snack lunch always arrange for hot soup, coffee or tea to be available. I still think with gratitude of the wife of John Cumberland, a forestry expert, who, in the days when we shot the moor, made it her special task to have hot soup ready for the lunch break. In late October, at 1,500 feet, conditions could be quite severe, and when we came down from the top butts and squeezed into the little hut she could have sold the stuff at £5 a cup.

A practice which I believe began in Norfolk and has now extended elsewhere is to pause for a hot drink at midday, then shoot through to about 2.30 p.m. and finish. This allows a leisurely lunch with no pressure to get on. The drawback is that it makes rather a sustained spell of activity for the older members, but it does solve the problem of the limited daylight available in December.

In some syndicates the lunch is included as part of the benefit from the subscription and traditionally the standard may be high. This is a possible source of economy and the members can be invited to decide between losing a course at lunch or fifty pheasants in the coverts.

It is obviously a duty of the shoot to ensure that the keeper, beaters and any other helpers are properly housed at lunch time. Whether you also feed them is up to you, but will be reflected in the pay. Turner, writing of the great Elveden shoot, paints a picture of days past, 'Luncheons for keepers, loaders and beaters were always brought out to a place previously decided on. To see the trestle tables piled high with stacks of both meat and cheese sandwiches all ready and laid out, would, I should think make the Minister of Foods nowadays scratch his head with both hands. Each sandwich about the size of a large plate would consist of more than a month's ration of meat and cheese today, and this was real British fare, no doctored bread, foreign meat, or "mouse-trap" cheese.'

My view is that a shoot should provide drink, say a bottle of beer apiece, but not food. This is not an expensive exercise but it helps the relationship I feel should exist between the beaters and the Guns. On the grouse moor we paid one of the beaters, normally a hill farmer, to run his tractor up to the lunch hut with a hydraulic scoop on the front. This we filled with beer and cartridge bags. At the end of each season I arranged a beaters' supper at the local pub, when vast shepherds' pies and much beer was consumed. They were a very decent bunch of Yorkshire dalesmen and we appreciated the miles they walked on our behalf. If you feel your beaters do a good job you also might consider the idea of an end of season beaters' supper. Always provided, that is, that you haven't adopted my suggestion of changing to dogs!

Although it is hardly a fault, I think it a flaw to see game tossed casually on the floor of a Land-Rover, where it quickly becomes ruffled, dirty and often squashed. The ideal is any form of game cart, but if this is not available it is a simple matter to contrive a few horizontal poles across a Land-Rover or a tractor.

When the day ends there comes the tricky matter of tipping the keeper; tricky because no one ever seems sure of how much to tip. In many syndicates the regular Guns do not tip, but the keeper receives a sizeable bonus at Christmas or the end of the season, which reflects the results. In practice it makes little difference whether each member gives a modest tip at each shoot, or whether everyone contributes equally to a single large payment. The advantage of the latter method is that it presents an opportunity to relate the reward to the results in a fairly dramatic way, and underlines the advantages of the keeper maintaining his efforts in the coming year. This system also overcomes the problem of the man who, left to his own initiative, would under-tip. Whether or not non-regular Guns should tip depends on the circumstances. A substitute Gun in a shoot which does not tip on each day has no real obligation to do so, for the permanent Gun will eventually make his full contribution. However, many a substitute will wish to tip and should not be discouraged. If you are shooting as a guest the easiest solution to the problem of how much, or so I have found, is to ask a regular Gun for local par. As a guide, at the time I write, there are no circumstances in which one would tip less than £2, and £3 is rapidly becoming the absolute minimum. Probably £2 plus £1 per hundred birds in the bag could be described as careful but not mean. By the time you read this the figures will be out of date, but may be of some help.

Before the Guns leave make sure they know the bag, and also maintain a careful record yourself. (Your lease will almost certainly require this.) The keeper will see that each Gun has a good, clean brace of pheasants, but I suggest you arrange matters so that Guns wanting more pay into the shoot account at the rate the birds would otherwise have fetched. This helps to reduce the *visible* cost of the shoot, and is more effective than reminding Guns who are grumbling about the cost that, besides the sport, they also had a lot of free game. It is also fairer to those members who, for various reasons, do not want much game and would otherwise be subsidising the larder of those that do.

In some ways organising the days when you do shoot is rather easier than the days when you do not. I have in mind when it rains. Not a season goes by but thousands of organisers, captains and owners are faced with a barn full of Guns and beaters, falling rain and a decision to be made. Do not guess – phone the Meteorological Office. In spite of the criticisms you hear, forecasts for the immediate future for local areas are usually accurate. If the man says it is going to rain heavily for most of the day, be decisive and cancel the shoot at once. If the forecast is uncertain and there is hope of a clearance then wait for it – do not start in heavy rain. Drizzle can be ignored but no matter how strong your intentions heavy rain will ruin the day. When there is a definite forecast of the rain clearing by, say, midday, it is best to announce that no shooting will begin before that time and give those with work to do a chance to nip away for an hour or so. It is a long morning in a cold, wet barn.

When the pheasant season ends the syndicate's sport is not necessarily over. If your woods provide roosting for pigeons this can give tremendous sport through February and March, the more so if neighbouring shoots can be persuaded to man their woods and keep the pigeons moving. The keener members can also be encouraged to help poke out the grey squirrel dreys.

Finally, arrange a shoot dinner. A long, informal affair when you can all look back with nostalgia to the days past and talk of dogs, birds and people. It is, after all, what shooting is all about.

5

On a Lesser Scale

This chapter is concerned with the laudable ambition of obtaining driven shooting at lower than normal costs, and I hope it will be useful to both the existing shoot organiser who is obliged to cut costs and the man forming a new shoot with the intention of shooting driven pheasants but with a limited budget. The ultimate in economy is to create a rough shoot, and I deal with this in Chapter 7. Whilst the prime object is saving money, it is also written in the belief that many shooting men enjoy involvement in all aspects of shooting. This is as well, for the first rule of saving money is greater personal involvement in the work. The chapter on keepers in my book, *Sportsman's Bag*, dwelt somewhat enviously on the life of a keeper – their outdoor existence and relative freedom from worry; the creative activities of building pens, traps and other devices in simple materials; the satisfaction of rearing young things and watching them mature. It is a way of life akin to a gardener's and just as wholesome. In practice, obliged to garden all week the pleasure would pall and I expect the same applies to gamekeeping. However, as I am proposing a dalliance rather than a marriage the truth is irrelevant.

Although I argued earlier that economies in high-class shoots should come from increased income rather than lower bags the time may come when a reduction is inevitable – a drop, as it were, from first to second division. At the lower end of the scale we may see what might be described as low-class driven change into high-class rough, and so on. Those who suffer this latter calamity may yet count their blessings for there are many virtues to rough shooting. Certainly it is healthier and it is no excuse to protest that you are too old; there are many different degrees of rough shooting and I always welcome an older Gun who is content to be placed as a strategic long-stop where he can both cut an escape route and have the occasional shot. The principal difference between driven and rough is that in the former the sport is brought to you and in the latter you have to go and find it, and a few former driven Guns may think wistfully of the good old days when their efforts were limited to adding two to their last number and finding the new peg. Most will welcome the new skills required – a knowledge of the ways of the quarry, of general fieldcraft, and the opportunity to work a dog which is seeking fresh game rather than retrieving a known runner. At heart I am a rough shooter and so are many others.

Undeniably the high cost of driven game shooting has restricted participation, with the exception of the farming community, to those either wealthy enough to pay or fortunate in their connections. Those shooting men coming from the farming community have maintained the old standards and attitudes, but some syndicates have been formed by town-based Guns who have fallen short, not by deliberate intent, but sheer lack of experience and guidance. In most cases the failings have been modest; for example, a keeper who, anxious to ensure a good bag among indifferent shots, has placed the pegs too close to the flushing points. In others, a few I think, but all diseases begin in a small way, there have been nasty rumours of 'instant' pheasants. Quite what constitutes an 'instant' pheasant I have never seen defined. Certainly it is not birds bought in at seven to eight weeks of age; whereas birds released a few days before a shoot very definitely are. A sensible definition would seem that an 'instant' pheasant has not had time to learn the neighbourhood, nor to recover its natural fear of man. My estimate is that a period of not less than eight weeks should pass between release and the first shoot.

As driven game shooting is inevitably an expensive business there will never be a time that the sport, at least in its more prolific form, is available to the less well-to-do, but one of the consequences of inflation is to make available good ground to those sportsmen who would previously have been out-bid by wealthier syndicates. Many syndicates drew the bulk of their members from the wealthier town-dwellers and these men are among the hardest hit by inflation. Landowners must now look over a wider range for their shooting tenants, and this is a healthy trend for the sport, which was becoming too confined and stereotyped. Even so landowners do not take this step willingly, for less well-off tenants will not be able to operate on the same scale and the bag must suffer. This, in turn, reduces the capital value of the sporting rights of the ground, which are related to the bag record. Whatever an owner might think of a wealthy syndicate's sporting attitudes, if they were prepared to pay a high rent and rear vast numbers of birds he could hardly afford to turn them away. Now, if they are not in the market he must look at others where knowledge and enthusiasm may offer some slight compensation for thinner purses. It is unlikely that when the Arabs rocketed the price of oil they realised their action might bring a new, and in some ways, better look to the face of British game shooting.

But enough of philosophising, let us turn to hard economies. In general all major cost reductions on larger shoots stem from one factor – the keeper. As we saw earlier he represents, on average 32·8 per cent of the cost of the shoot and to maintain him whilst reducing the scale of his activities is usually illogical. I write 'usually', because on good ground it may make sense to cut rearing costs and let the keeper spend more time helping the wild birds. However, this policy will only achieve a modest reduction as the main overheads are unchanged. Any major economy can only come from employing a part-time keeper and the remainder of this chapter is divided into the two possibilities:

1. The part-time keeper.
2. Self-help – that is where the functions of the keeper are, so far as possible, carried out by the members of the shoot.

On the 'half loaf being better than none' theory I will begin with the part-time keeper. Shoots functioning with this arrangement are often composed of optimists who expect to have their shooting cake and eat it. The arrangement can vary between a disaster and a great success – it all depends on the part-time keeper. The profession has some fine men but it also has some layabouts and one of the difficulties of employing a keeper efficiently is what I call the 'no bricks laid quandary'. In other words if you employ a bricklayer his performance can be judged by counting the number of bricks laid, but so much of the work of a keeper cannot be quantified over a few months. By the end of a season you should know your man well, and after two or three seasons very well, but after a few months a precise assessment is impossible. I have sad memories of a part-time keeper I employed in Sussex who performed well throughout the rearing season and, when I disappeared to Scotland in August, had a thousand poults divided between two release pens. I returned in September to a mountain of office work and, in the belief that all was well, contented myself with occasional telephone chats. When we shot the main wood in November it contained two pheasants and a fox! Investigation showed he had failed to carry out any normal keepering procedures, and I suspect one or two other decidedly unkeeper-like activities had gone on. Naturally he was dismissed at once but it was an expensive failure and, fundamentally, the fault was mine. Keepers are human and only a minority of humans actually enjoy work. Left to their own devices most people do no more than they have to, and if you are to get the best from a keeper it is usually necessary to make regular tours of the ground with him. This principle applies whether you have a good part-time keeper or an indifferent one. The better man will be pleased with your interest and will work through pride, and the lesser man will work through fear of being found wanting.

The post of part-time keeper can be well filled by a retired keeper, if his health is reasonable. Equally the job can be done by a man of only limited experience if he has common sense and energy. The overriding factor is that a part-timer has not time to do the job properly, and shortcomings are inevitable. Your problem is to see he makes the best use of the limited time available.

I once set out in *The Field* the revolutionary argument that a shoot could have better results by dispensing with many keepering activities and buying in seven-week poults instead. So far as large-scale shoots are concerned, this is an interesting theoretical exercise rather than a practical proposal, but for 'lesser scale' shoots there are distinct possibilities. For large shoots the reasoning was that rearing 4,000 pheasants would cost, over and above the keeper's wages, etc., about £3,000. If we add to this the approximate cost of the keeper we have a further £3,000, making a total of £6,000. By dispensing with the keeper and buying 4,000 poults at, say, £1 each, there is a saving of £2,000 and although some of this will have to be spent on part-time keepering from the time of the poults' arrival, and for feeding through the season, there is still a good margin. This arrangement would fail where the ground is good, and the full-time presence of a keeper is essential for the wild stock to breed successfully. However, on poor ground, and particularly where the surrounding ground is unkeepered and vermin is rife, the wild stock will be low even with a keeper's help, and there is a good argument for saving his wages during the spring and summer and using the money to buy poults. The hard fact is that money spent in wages *may* mean more pheasants, but money spent on poults unquestionably *does*.

Of course, this reasoning is shallow and ignores the numerous other reasons for maintaining a full-time keeper on large-scale shoots. I propound it partly because one day it may be a measure forced on us by costs, but mainly because the basic reasoning will make sense for many 'lesser scale' shoots. Let us put some figures to the theory. If you have to pay £60 a month for keepering, over the six months from February to July inclusive you will spend £360. With this you could be certain of putting some 300 poults into the release pens and there is little point in employing a part-time keeper over this period unless you are confident his presence will result in a greater number of wild birds. It is all a question of the ground. With good ground it will be worth while – with poor ground it is unlikely. Remember the trapping efforts of a part-time keeper will make little difference if you are surrounded by unkeepered ground.

The practice of releasing poults on to unkeepered ground is open to criticism, but with care the risks are not too great. The factor often overlooked is that most British predators are only dangerous to eggs and chicks; the main threat to poults of seven weeks and upwards is the fox. The keeper should be employed for a fortnight before the birds arrive and concentrate on two tasks – overhauling the release pens and eliminating foxes. (Except in those areas where a reasonable fox population is maintained for the benefit of the Hunt.) Both these tasks are dealt with later, and, if done well, the poults have little to fear. Of course some will die of predators or exposure within the first few weeks, but the majority will survive. (The usual estimate is that about a third die in this early period.)

The death-rate among artificially reared pheasant chicks is small, about 10 per cent depending on the quality of management, but this is of no consequence to the man who buys seven-week poults – he has, on the ground, the actual number he orders. But the death-rate among wild pheasant chicks from hatching to seven weeks is very high indeed. Taking it as 75 per cent then to rear 100 poults to seven weeks of age the wild stock will have to hatch 400. Returning to my earlier figures, which suggested 300 poults could be purchased with money saved from wages, it follows that the wild hatch would have to increase by 1,200 chicks merely to break even – a most unlikely result just from the efforts of a part-time keeper.

There is, of course, no fundamental reason why you should not rear your own birds by using a part-time keeper. His limited hours will mean fewer numbers, but this would accord with the policy of conducting the whole shoot on a lesser scale. The major problem is that, as a part-timer is only present spasmodically, unless he can rear at his own home, or at the home of one of the shoot members, the young chicks are left unattended at their most vulnerable age. Various arrangements are possible, including letting one of the shoot members do the rearing in return for a reduced subscription. Whatever alternative you adopt do look at the price of seven-week poults, and unless you show a worth while saving reflect whether the difference is worth the risks. If you buy poults you must finish up with the correct number, but if you rear, a disaster could mean the cost per bird is much higher. Of course this finely balanced situation exists only where you are paying for the labour content of rearing; in a 'self-help' syndicate it is unquestionably cheaper to rear.

Another snag with a part-time keeper is the shoot's vulnerability to poaching, for no part-timer can be expected to mount night watches – at least not on a regular basis. As you will have fewer birds in the coverts than a large shoot, the temptation for poachers is reduced, but they are still a threat. Just how much varies from area to area but, on balance, poaching is less serious than it was early in the century. The prime motive for poaching is financial, and wages have gone up and pheasant prices down. At the same time the steady flow of labour to the cities means that fewer men know how to poach. I am not minimising the problem – I have suffered badly within the last few months –

but I repeat that poaching is not as bad as it was, and certainly when keepers and poachers meet there is less violence.

The near-universal possession of motor cars has brought a large increase in petty poaching by people not resident in the area. The common practice is to creep along a quiet road, knock over a bird with a ·22 rifle or a gun, retrieve it and drive off. Irritating as this practice is, it is no more. I know the head and beat keepers on a fine Cambridgeshire estate, and when I meet them there is usually a tale of a 'hit-and-run' raid. The teller will pinken with wrath at the vileness of the scoundrel who stole a pheasant, which is a little unbalanced when you consider the annual bag rarely falls below 6,000.

Having looked at the problems which go with the employment of a part-time keeper we can now consider the economies. Obviously saving money on the keeper is only a first, if major, step in a general scaling down. There is little saving, and no point, in merely affecting a modest reduction of some 10–15 per cent as against the cost of a large shoot. Unless the whole organisation is reduced proportionately the usual result is a large drop in the bag for only a small reduction in cost.

Logically the next reduction is the area of ground. It is always difficult to be specific on areas as quality is so important. But given average ground 1,000 acres is enough, and 500 acres of good ground will make an excellent small shoot. All the advice given previously on leases applies, but if the owner has previously let to a more highpowered syndicate, or is splitting what was one large shoot into two smaller, he may be reluctant to grant a long-term lease until he sees your performance. This is reasonable, and in your modest financial position you too will probably prefer to have a trial year or so, but immediately you are content seek a longer lease. If you are dealing with an owner who has previously leased on a higher plane he may want to impose a rearing obligation in the lease. Make sure the number is realistic.

The procedure for finding your fellow Guns is the same, except that you should seek enthusiasts who are willing (and able) to help. The extent to which you call upon their efforts will vary according to the form of shoot you plan. You may simply require Guns to supplement the beaters as occasional walking Guns or, at the other extreme, members might be required actually to work at peak times in the rearing season. Whatever level of participation you require should be borne in mind when you select your members, and their obligations should be made clear at the beginning.

Remember also that members of 'lesser scale' shoots are less likely to be free to shoot on weekdays and the availability of beaters on Saturdays needs checking.

On a 'lesser scale' shoot you have more flexibility than your high-powered contemporaries, who are rather committed to an all-or-nothing situation. At the top end you might aim for an annual bag of 1,000, and this might be achieved by putting down 2,500 and expecting to shoot some 30–35 per cent with the balance made up by wild birds. The possible costings might run: ground £1,000; rates £250; keeper £750 (not necessarily paid on a regular weekly basis); pheasants £2,500; corn £500; beaters £500; and extras £500. This total of £6,000 represents a reduction of some £4,000–5,000 on the current costs of a major shoot, and if shared between nine Guns is approximately £666 each.

The pleasure of the Guns does not vary in strict accord with the bag, which is to say that provided they get enough sport they are happy, and they are not a great deal happier if the bag is doubled or trebled. Therefore, if your aim is to keep everyone happy at minimum cost it is worth examining the bag necessary to achieve 'satisfaction level'. It is higher than you might think. Given an annual bag of 1,000, shot by nine Guns on ten days, each Gun will average eleven birds a day. Assuming eight drives a Gun will have several blanks and, at the best, a few drives of two or three. Not exactly prolific when compared to the old days. (Turner records that, on the Elveden Estate, three Guns killed over 600 partridges in a day, and on 8 September 1876, the Maharajah Duleep Singh killed 780 to his own gun.) A 2,000 annual bag only doubles these expectations. This is where rough shooting scores; as each bird has to be worked for success is more satisfying. It also eliminates the boredom of a poor day's driven shooting when an eternity passes between each bird.

Although eleven birds a day may not be prolific sport neither is it, at £666, very cheap. We will go down the scale even further. Let the ground rent be £750, either because the acreage is smaller or the quality poorer. Assume the rates are £150 and that we must limit the cost of the keeper to £500. The hours we will get for £10 per week are inadequate at peak times so it becomes inevitable that his employment will vary with the season. The case for buying in seven-week poults becomes very strong, the more so if our man is a river keeper, or some other countryman who is busy in the summer and slack in the winter. (A cheaper alternative would be to pay your part-timer to rear day-old chicks at his home.) Let us presume that £1,000 is spent on pheasants and this produces 1,000 seven-week poults; suppose the figure spent on beaters is £250 – an impossible figure for it represents only five men a day at £5 each for ten days. Five beaters will not, of course, do, but we are now slumming and you must either send your loved ones into the beating line or use dogs. Suppose the corn is £300 and the extras £150 – a total of £3,100. Divided between nine Guns this is

c

approximately £344 each. With luck the bag might be 500; that is, five or six a day per Gun. To shoot these a Gun will probably have double the number in range, but even so I think half-a-dozen birds per Gun per day is about as low as the bag can go without becoming rather farcical.

It is important not to look for miracles. Good planning and management will produce more pheasants for a given outlay, but there is no escaping the relationship between money spent and birds bagged. There are many shooting men whose circumstances make the expenditure of even £300 or so a year impossible. In theory their solution is to turn to rough shooting but this is not the only answer. There has long been an erroneous belief that game shooting was either driven or rough shooting, and that if a man could not afford the first then the delights of the very testing targets of driven game were denied him and he had to be content with rough shooting. This sharp distinction was no more accurate than believing that all marriages are either intensely happy or dismal failures, for the different forms of shooting have never been so clearly defined and there have always been a large number of shoots which fall into neither category. Whilst rough shoots, in the sense that no keeper is employed and the members do all the work of the shoot, they are driven in that the conduct of shooting days follows the normal pattern of a driven shoot and most of the bag is shot by standing Guns. For want of a better name I will refer to these as self-help syndicates.

Before leaving driven shoots on a lesser scale and moving to 'self-helps', several other points warrant attention. If several local shoots have been hit financially it is worth considering sharing a full-time keeper between two or three. He will not, of course, be able to do his job properly, but better this than an inexperienced man for you and a lost job for him.

Any shoot functioning with a part-timer needs to look hard at its feeding procedures, for the ideal of a keeper whistling birds into the feed rides is probably unattainable. However, you must use the best techniques circumstances permit to keep the birds at home. A subsequent chapter deals with feeding, but the Game Conservancy booklet *Game on the Farm* goes into greater detail and should be required reading. The automatic feeders which dispense corn at pre-set times, whilst ringing a bell to attract the birds, are the next best thing to a keeper and almost certainly are now a permanent feature of the game shooting scene.

Rearing with a part-timer often means that chicks must be left for several hours at a stretch. In these conditions propane gas or paraffin are a more reliable source of heat than electricity.

Finally we reach 'self-help', in which the followers personally carry out all the activities of rearing, keepering and beating which would normally be done by paid employees. On the most modest levels we find simple rough shoots where a few birds are reared to supplement the wild stock, but at the other extreme it is possible to operate a successful small driven shoot in which the birds, although limited in numbers, give every bit as much sport as in large shoots and at a fraction of the cost. Although this advice is intended for the more ambitious level of self-help shoots much of it can be adapted to others. For those considering a shoot on these lines do not be deterred by the prospect of the work – it is enormous fun and very satisfying. Not everyone will agree but this should be ascertained before he joins the shoot. Self-help game shooting can never be as 'pure' a sport as wildfowling or pigeon-shooting, but some of the sense of achievement exists. One of the reasons we shoot is to satisfy the age-old hunting instinct, and it takes a strong imagination to convince your primitive self that it is enough to stand at a peg and kill passing pheasants.

This section is unashamedly for the impecunious, whose prime purpose is the maximum sport at the least cost. I will assume that most readers would prefer a shoot in which at least some of the birds shot are driven. The view that walked-up birds are all easy is a fallacy, but they do present a different form of shot and a mixture of walked-up and driven offers a splendid variety. With this in view let us go back to the three essentials for driven pheasants – ground, birds and beaters. The beaters can be ignored, for the birds will be driven by some of the syndicate members, assisted by their dogs and various human helpers.

The ground remains the major problem and its discovery is no easier at this minor level. Financially you are not competing with conventional syndicates but the demand for smaller shoots is intense. You can, however, offer the owner an advantage over most other bidders, for the majority will wish to harvest without sowing. Any sensible owner will welcome a mini-syndicate with plans to improve the ground, and your advertisements and other approaches should proclaim your intentions.

There is one possibility which can both produce the ground and solve some of the keepering problems in one stroke. Writing of grander syndicates I suggested the involvement of the owner or farmer in the shoot was of doubtful advantage – it could work well but it might create grave problems. When money is not the major problem safety is the wiser course, but at the self-help level the advantages greatly outweigh the risk of incompatibility. Ideally you want an owner, or farming tenant, in possession of the sporting rights, who wants to shoot but lacks the time or the knowledge to organise a syndicate. In the case of a farming owner he is more likely to lack time than knowledge, and one can understand a farmer who would rather let someone else do all the work. The other possibility, of an owner who lacks knowledge, crops up less frequently, but it is there. In either case a fair arrangement is that you form a syndicate, and run it, and the owner takes a free Gun or Guns in return for providing the ground. Whether he gets one free Gun or more depends upon the value of the ground he owns, how many paying Guns there are, and how much they spend upon providing the sport.

The advantages are manifold. Properly arranged, the owner will be keeping the sporting rights and it is possible no rates will be payable. He can provide corn; supply a trailer and a few beaters; vary the positions of his crops to favour the shooting; put in cover crops and is constantly around as a deterrent to poachers. He will not, of course, supply all these services without charge, but the cost to him will not be great, and if paid by an extra Gun or two the cost to the syndicate will be modest.

However you solve the ground problem, remember you cannot be fussy if you can only afford a low rent. This is a major reason for forming a modest syndicate rather than a rough shoot of two or three people, for the rental ability of the former is higher. In general a modest syndicate should mean more ground, more birds, more dog work, more companions and more fun. Granted the greater number of birds will be shared between more Guns but the greater efficiency of the larger team should mean a bigger average.

The need for a properly prepared lease for the ground is no less than for more superior shoots, although the difficulty of persuading the owner to see this may be greater. However there is not the same requirement to evidence your relationship with your fellow Guns so fully for, as everyone is a worker, if the results are disappointing it is as much their fault as yours. Even so you would be wise to take the ground in your name, for you then have some measure of control. With a small shoot at a modest rent the risk of losing your Guns and being left with the rent baby is much less.

With the ground leased and the syndicate formed the next step is deciding on the management policy. This may seem excessively grand for a modest enterprise, but although the details will be simple it is always wise before commencing any task to consider exactly what you are trying to achieve and the resources at your disposal. Failing this you can easily finish up finding you have spent too much of the annual income on rearing and not left enough for winter feeding, or some comparable mix-up.

The volume of keepering done will depend on the skill of the members and the time they have available. You will be wise to

9. The most certain way of obtaining high, sporting pheasants is to drive them over tall trees. (Note the lead given by the Gun.)

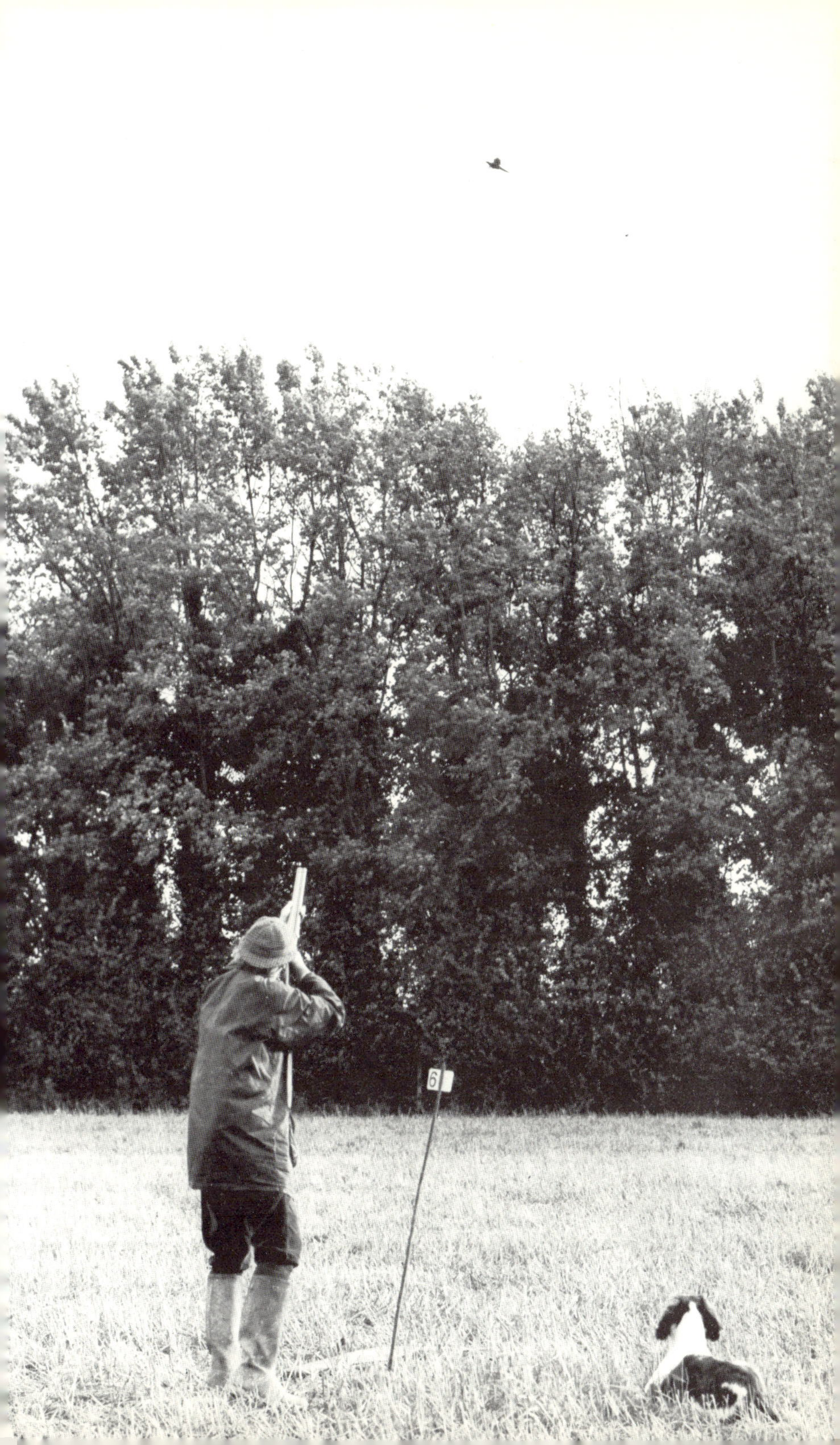
6

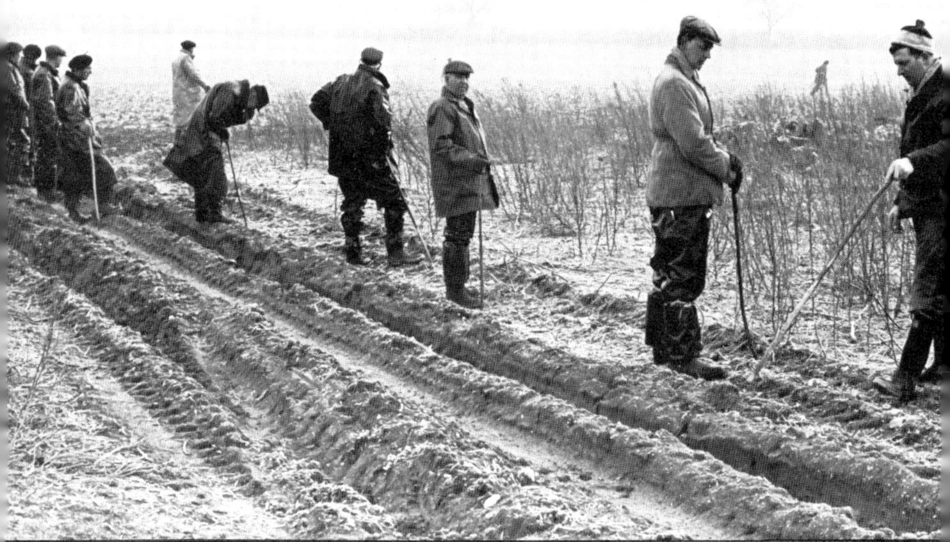

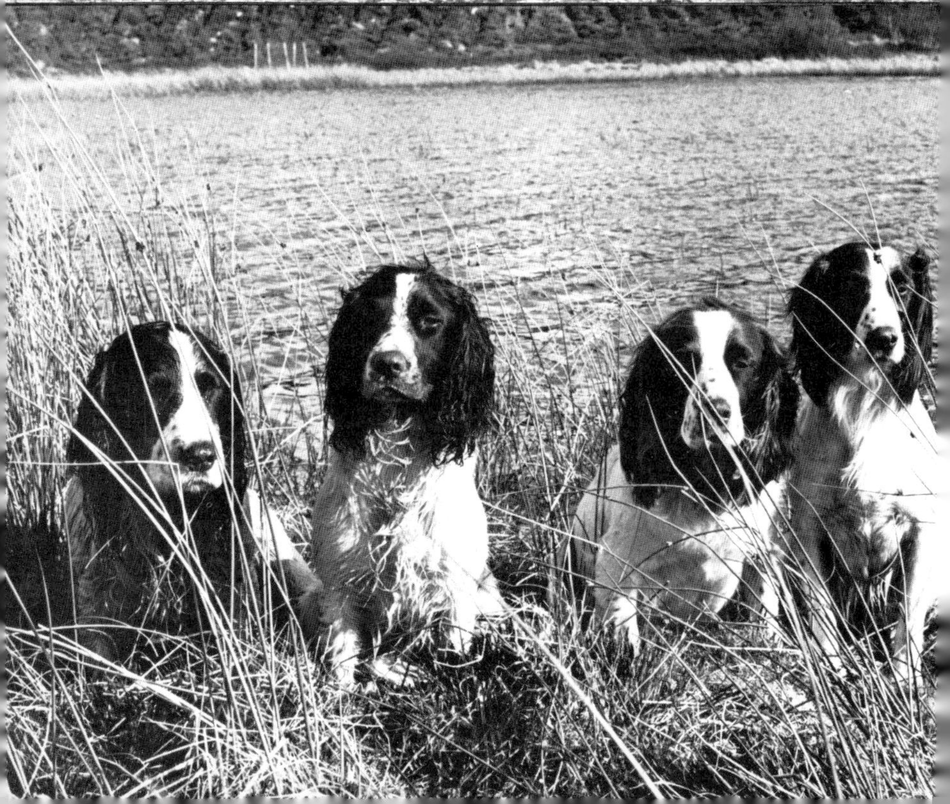

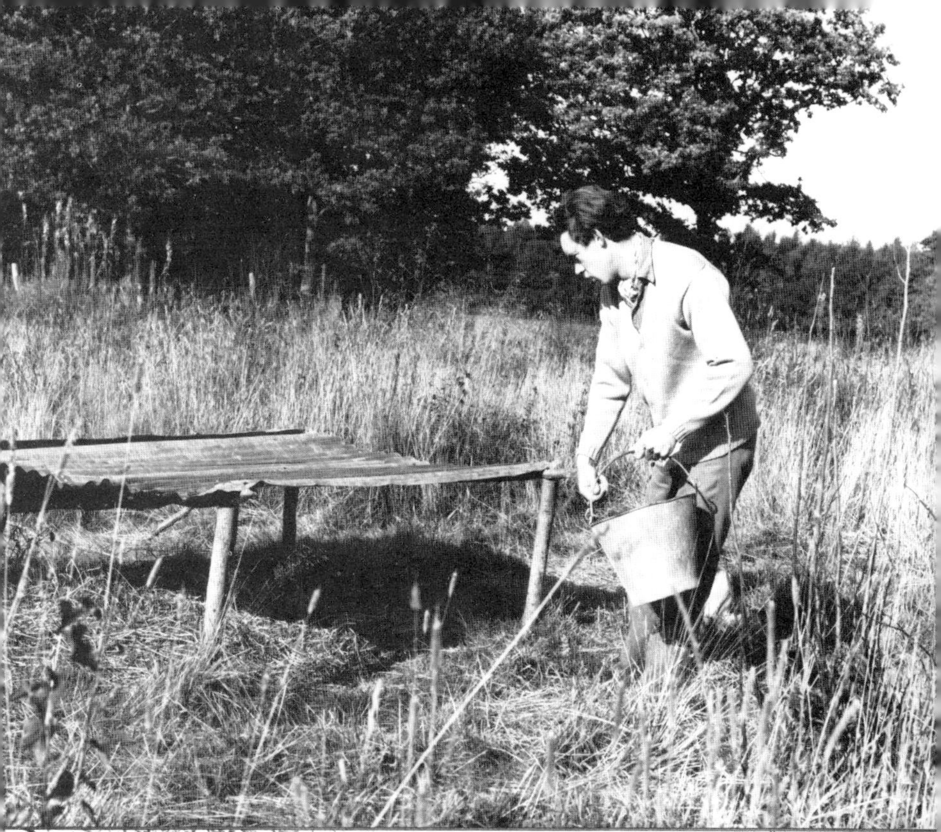

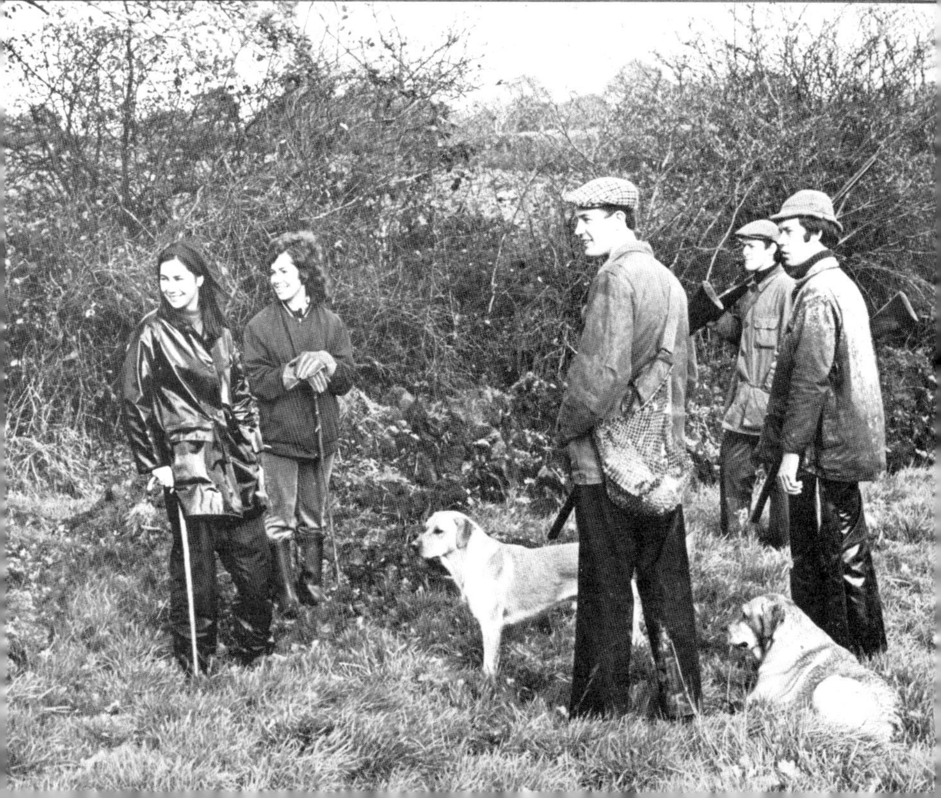

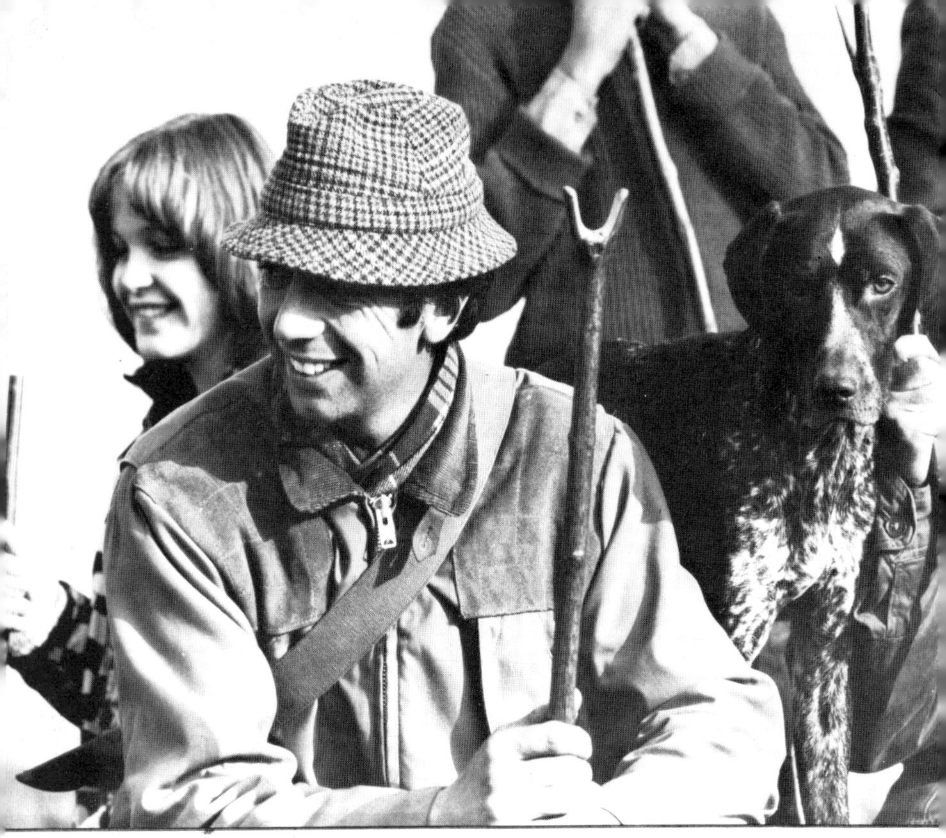
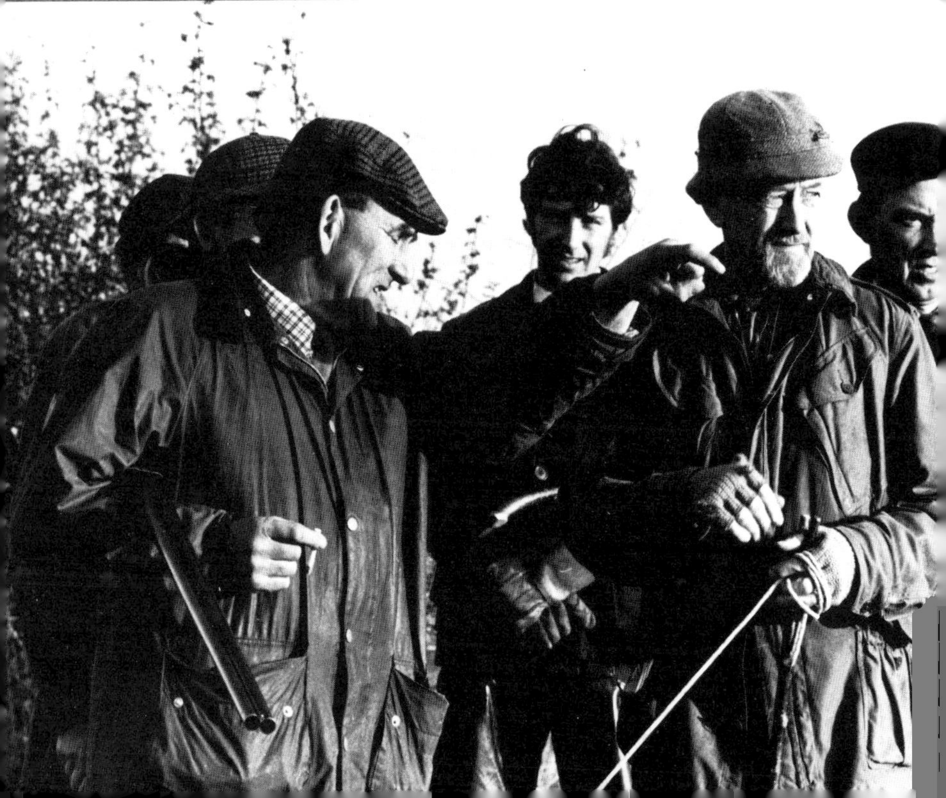

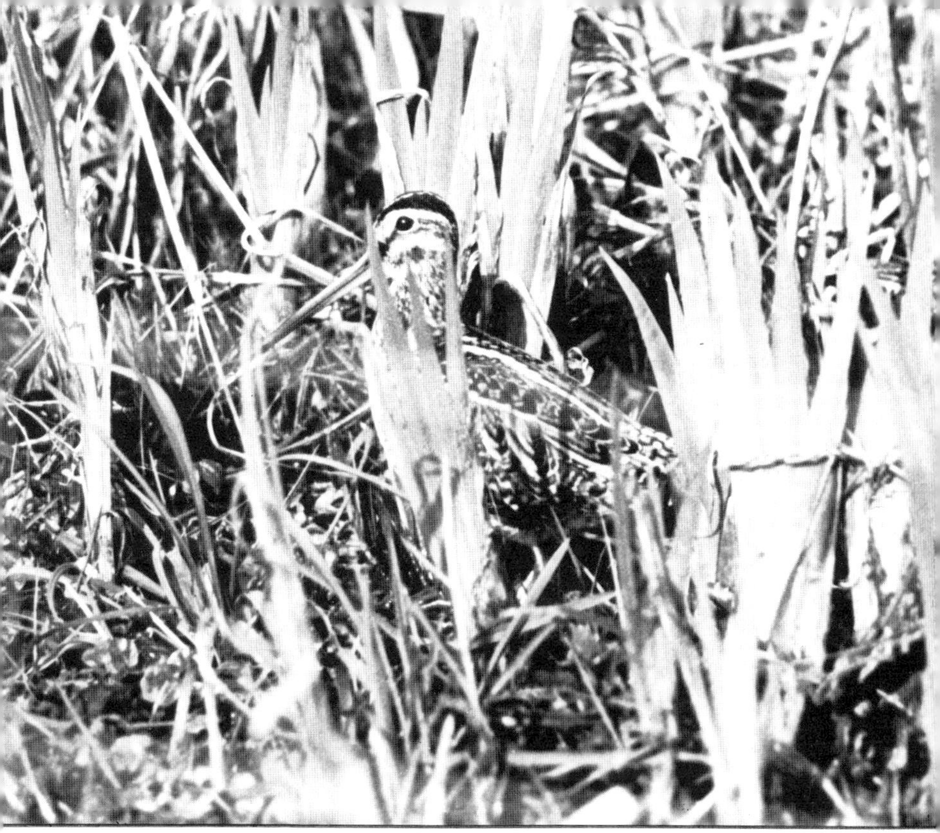

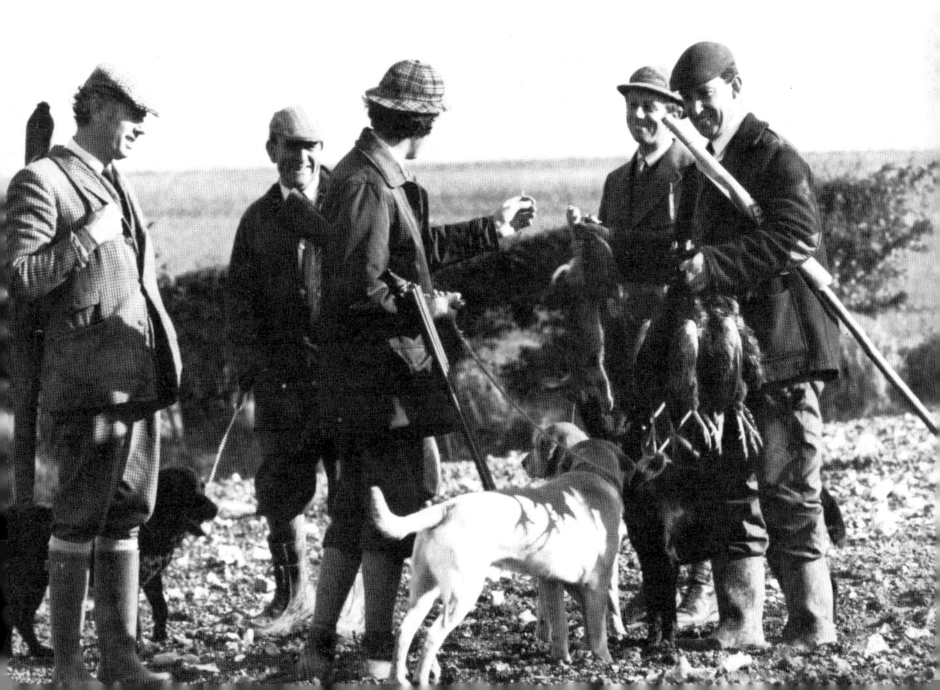

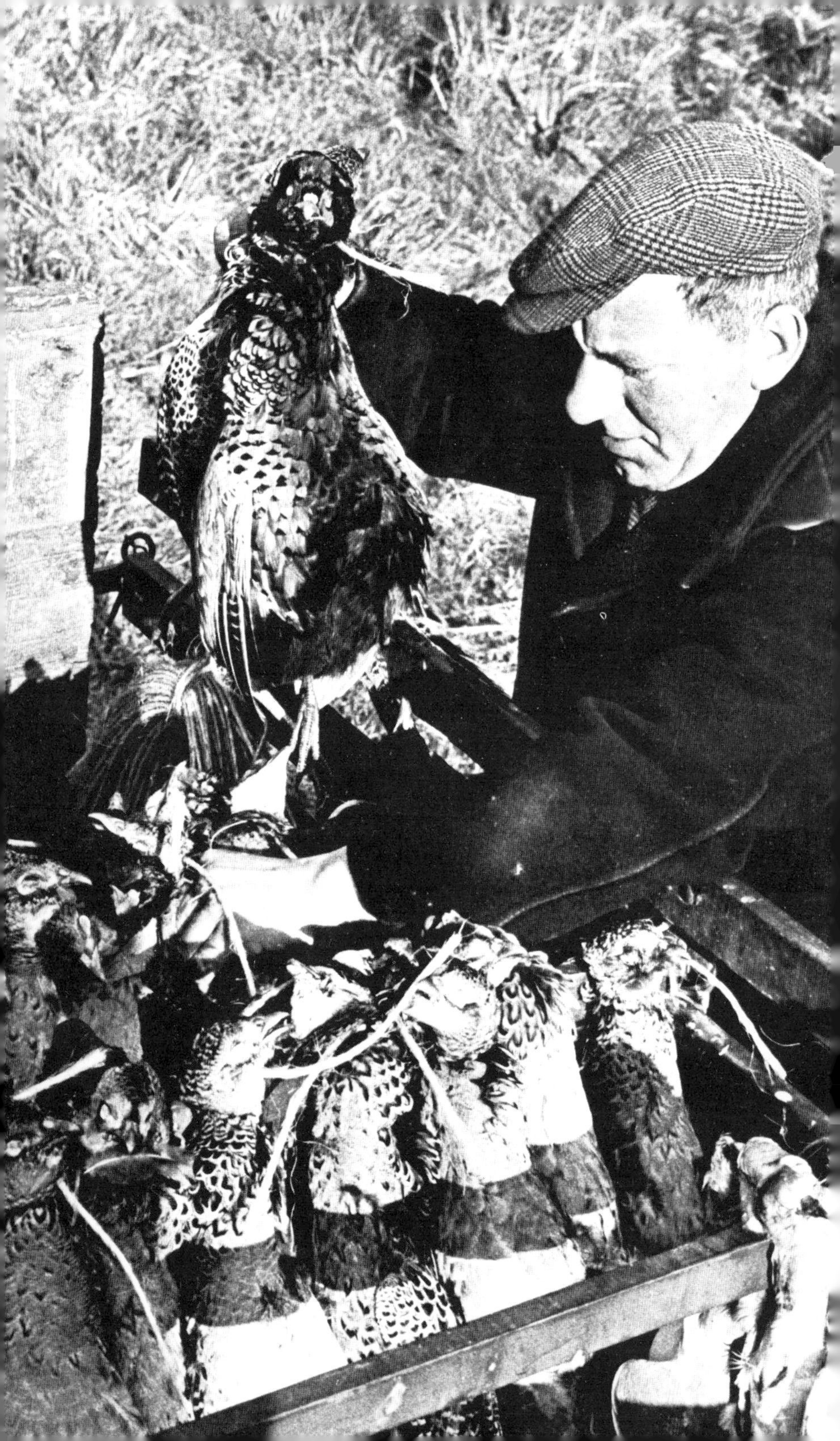

assume limited skills and much less time applied than forecast in the first flush of enthusiasm.

Rearing remains a sound investment. Writing of large shoots I argued that the cost of rearing more birds was small compared to the basic overheads, and that reducing the numbers reared achieved little economy and much reduced the sport. In a self-help shoot the basic overheads are low and producing extra birds is proportionately more expensive, but it is still sense to rear the maximum finances permit and the ground will hold. In practice, if the members rear the pheasants and the bag is sold well, the net cost of each bird will represent excellent sporting value.

Suggestions on rearing with particular relevance to 'home' rearing appear later, but I do urge you to mark each bird, either with a wing-tag or a leg-ring. Without this precaution you will have no idea of the results obtained from your released birds or their behaviour, and may go on year after year wasting effort and money. The actual percentage you bag is obviously the prime factor, but other information is important; for example, the variation in results from different release pens. I have tried being very scientific and using individually numbered tags noting the pen and the date of release of each bird. Unfortunately in the rush and bustle of a shooting day it has proved difficult to note the drive in which every tag has appeared and I now find I learn more by the simpler system of allocating a different colour of leg-ring or wing-tag to each pen.

Although self-help syndicates can pay for either rearing labour or seven-week poults, both would be quite contrary to the enterprise, and the practice of rearing by members is almost universal. This can either be done at a central spot, with different members being responsible for set periods, or for several members each to rear separate batches. The latter eliminates the risk of a mass disaster. A convenient division of work is that one group rears, and another takes over at the release pen stage and carries on for some weeks. There is no reason why those members with more money and restricted time should not pay more and work less, and vice versa. The cost of the rearing equipment can be kept down by rearing two batches of birds each season, and this also eliminates the risk of losing a large proportion of the year's rearing to one misfortune, for example, an outbreak of disease.

In the chapter that dealt with rearing, I stress there is nothing to be learnt that does not already appear in the publications of the Game Conservancy. A careful study of their present booklets, backed up by any new works they produce, will be sufficient for even a novice to rear pheasants successfully. There would be little point in my mentioning the technicalities except that the Game Conservancy have

18. Even a simple arrangement such as this prevents game being trampled on the floor of a Land-Rover or trailer.

hardly anticipated the problems that beset those amateurs who have to rear under far from ideal conditions, sometimes quite literally, in their own back gardens. As I annually rear several hundred birds in my own garden I feel qualified to give advice on this rather specialised branch. In planning your rearing bear in mind one salient point – it is far harder to turn an egg into a day-old chick than to turn a day-old into a seven-week poult. Hatching your own eggs also means either the problems and labour of broody hens; the expense of an incubator; or paying someone else to hatch. If you have doubts about either your team's ability or the extent of the money saved, I suggest you buy day-olds.

The space problem in rearing usually comes not because there is no spare ground on the shoot, but through time forcing the individuals to rear at home. It is possible to rise early, tend 200 chicks and still catch the 8.20, but not if the shoot is any distance. Given a sensible and obedient wife the arrangement even has the advantage of a resident assistant keeper, although even the best can become a trifle short when they are giving a dinner party for eight in an hour and a flock of ten-day-old chicks refuse to enter the brooder house quietly.

Constant rearing on one area of ground invites disease, and if at all possible the position of the rearing pen should be changed annually. Unfortunately, few modern gardens permit this and, in this event, it is best to build a permanent rearing pen. After each year's programme is completed the ground cover should be cleared and the entire pen area and a yard strip outside the pen liberally sprayed with one of the heavy-duty germicides available from the various game farmers. This should be repeated shortly before the new chicks are introduced the following year. The Game Conservancy suggests that 200 chicks need a pen of 900 square feet, moved once. That is 1,800 square feet from hatching to transfer to the release pens. I use a permanent pen of 1,300 square feet and although, for safety's sake, I now use plastic anti-peck bits, feather picking has never been a problem. This may be due to providing ample cover, partly by encouraging wild brambles, and partly with cut branches laid on the pen floor in the early spring to provide support to the developing natural cover. A major problem of suburban pheasant rearers is not foxes but cats, who will stick a paw through conventional netting. I use ½-inch mesh at the bottom, dug in 1 foot, and then 1-inch mesh from 3 feet upwards. The roof is of plastic net. The gap between the arrival of the first and second batch is only four weeks, and the first batch must harden quickly so that it can roost outside and free the brooder house in time for the new arrivals. This I find no problem, although I provide corrugated, clear-plastic shelters in case of very wet weather. The rapid growth of ability of young pheasants to stand low night temperatures and rain is surprising, but the basic rule for the first week or so is to keep them warm.

Shooting day organisation for self-help syndicates follows the same pattern as conventional syndicates, but a few extra points require attention. Beating is a constant problem, for the money left in the shoot account will all be destined for feeding. A few youngsters may be employed at slave rates, plus a large sandwich lunch, but the bulk of the beating must be done either by volunteers, dogs or the Guns themselves. The theory is that the Guns take it in turns to drive or stand. In practice, those with dogs usually drive and those without stand. Silence is particularly important, as few self-help shoots have enough man (or woman) power to provide stops in advance of each drive. The removal, with permission, of a short section of hedge, or the erection of a length of wire netting helps cut escape routes.

Fair play among the driving Guns is called for if birds flying forward are to reach the standing Guns. Safety is more of a problem than in formal shoots, which do not have the tricky situation of armed men facing one another. Personally I ban shooting at all ground game.

The earlier remarks on winter feeding apply but as the strength of self-help syndicates is the availability of unpaid labour there is no reason why feeding should not be carried out efficiently. A useful tip is to establish storage containers for the corn at strategic positions around the shoot. If these can be filled early in the season, and before the wet weather arrives, the task of regular hopper maintenance is eased.

As I stressed earlier the pattern of all these 'lesser scale' shoots varies considerably – they are all essentially exercises in personal ingenuity. However, there are many examples scattered throughout the country which prove they work very well.

The brief details of two within my personal experience may be useful. One operates near Dorking, only a few miles south of where the great, unbroken sprawl of suburban London ends. There are, I think, only five permanent members, including the farmer on the ground and the local vet who assumes responsibility for the rearing programme. All work, and expenses are shared. The annual bag is about 500, shot efficiently by an obviously happy team, for whom the actual shooting is merely the high point of the year and not the sport in itself.

The second is a small 300 acre shoot I organise and run personally, together with the farm manager who has a Gun for his efforts. It lies in a not very suitable part of Surrey, rather over-wooded, and with little or no cereal grown. The arrangement is the happy one I mentioned earlier where the ground owner charges no rent, but lets me organise the shooting and keeps several Guns for his friends. The value of this illustration is the sport that can come from even very part-time efforts, for I am involved in several other shoots and have numerous other commitments.

In the season before this arrangement began the ground yielded about a dozen birds. Three seasons have now passed and the improvement can be seen from the details of last season. I reared some 400 pheasants at home, and eventually released 362 in two batches into three release pens, all carefully sited. They were kept quiet, fed and watered, and when they began to wander should have found at least some of the fifteen feed-points with feed hoppers and straw, protected by corrugated asbestos roofs and wind-breaks of straw bales. Daily feeding was impossible but the hoppers were kept topped up.

We shot on eight days, beating with the previously suggested mixture of Guns, relatives and small boys. The bag, ignoring the 'various', was 193 of which ninety-six were wild and ninety-seven reared, one being from the previous season. At first sight the result might be considered rather disappointing, with only a 26·8 per cent return on reared birds. In fact, as the national average is about 36 per cent, this return from a virtually unkeepered shoot is very satisfactory. Nor is it sufficient to sum up matters by concluding that the efforts doubled the bag – they did considerably more, for without the feed points the numbers of wild birds would be well down. (In fact they are almost certainly not wild birds but untagged reared birds from nearby shoots. However, as they will shoot at least 25 per cent of my birds my conscience is clear.)

The total cost of rearing the birds, including propane gas and wing-tags, but excluding capital depreciation on rearing equipment, was £170. Many small items were saved – for example, water troughs were made from car tyres, and the poults were transported in stout cardboard boxes instead of hampers. Corn cost £90, and oddments another £15. This total of £275 averages out at £1·42 per pheasant – far lower than usual. The average bag was twenty-four pheasants, which with seven Guns shooting meant 3·5 birds per Gun/day.

Whether or not you regard a day in which you shoot three or four pheasants, and spend part of it as a beating Gun, as pleasurable, depends on you. Personally, although in the course of a season I shoot with a variety of private shoots and syndicates in several counties, I always return to my little Surrey shoot with keen anticipation, and this is shared by my guests, some of whom normally experience prolific sport. Whatever your personal views, the fact remains that with a little ingenuity it is still possible to have a great deal of sporting fun at low cost.

6

Keepers and Keepering

It is not the object of this chapter to give detailed advice on predator control, rearing, releasing, feeding and all the other aspects of the keeper's work. To attempt this in so little space would be ridiculous and would, in any event, only duplicate many previous and excellent works. The contemporary problem is not knowing what the keeper should do, but deciding the priorities for his limited time. Few shoots nowadays can afford to employ more than one keeper and he cannot possibly do everything that, ideally, he should. Given this situation the task of the shoot organiser is to ensure that the keeper is cost-effective – in other words produces the maximum results for the minimum cost. It is unfortunate that we have to think of our sport in such commercial terms, but we have no choice.

The need to plan carefully, so that limited resources of time and money go on the right priorities, applies just as much to syndicates operating on either a part-time keeper or a self-help basis. Obviously different shoots will have different needs and problems, but, if nothing more, I hope this chapter will encourage shoot organisers to think in terms of cost effectiveness.

For detailed advice I would recommend the following Game Conservancy booklets: *Game on the Farm*; *Game and Shooting Crops* (No. 2); *Partridge Rearing* (No. 4); *Pheasant Rearing* (No. 8); and *Forestry and Pheasants* (No. 15).

These publications are packed with wisdom and it is no exaggeration to suggest that if their recommendations are applied with common sense and industry the results must be good, disasters excepted.

It is logical to start with the business of finding the keeper, be he full-time or part-time. The qualities you should seek in a keeper were most admirably assessed by F. G. Stanfield in *Syndicate Shooting*, when he said he must have a thorough technical knowledge of his work, integrity, tact and human understanding, and organising ability.

Undeniably this is what you want. What you get may not exactly conform – indeed, if it does you are exceptionally lucky for, as in most areas of employment, sensible employers keep good men. It is, therefore, essential that you take up references, preferably by telephone, for men will speak their criticisms far more freely than they will write them. While it is important to check that an applicant knows keepering thoroughly the likelihood is, provided he has had several years experience, that he will. The greater problem is to assess whether he has the character to do the job properly, or whether drink, matrimonial trouble, sheer idleness or any other human failings will prevent him. In your discussion with his previous employer you must probe a little below the surface. Although a man may have been pleased to part with his keeper he may, for various reasons ranging from sympathy to a guilt complex, wish to paint his character as white as possible. Asking if the keeper knows how to operate an incubator may, therefore, bring a truthful affirmative. Taking the question a stage further, and inquiring whether he may be absolutely relied upon to do the job, could bring a different answer.

Conversely a critical reference from a past employer may not always be accurate. In a clash between a difficult, overbearing employer and plain-spoken, independently minded keeper, the keeper always loses, but properly managed, he could be an excellent man.

It is not sufficient to decide that a keeper suits you and then offer him the post. There are two sides to the relationship, and if it is to last you must also consider whether you and the job suit the keeper. You will be wise to discuss your plans and ideas with him to gauge his reaction. Older men, in particular, may lack flexibility and if a shoot is to operate economically the keeper must be prepared to try out new methods and techniques as they appear. If you represent a syndicate your own position is not over-strong, for syndicates are less permanent employers than estates or large farms.

The traditional time for a keeper to change his job is the beginning of February, but those seeking a move will be sniffing the wind from October onwards. Most sensible men will find their new position before vacating the old, and a man who has either given or received notice before you interview him arrives with a question mark as to his common sense, if nothing more. The usual channel of contact is the classified advertisement columns of the sporting press and, here again, you should put in a fairly extensive advertisement. The Gamekeepers' Association, now incorporated with WAGBI, also provides a register of keepers seeking positions. However, when all is said, nothing beats a personal recommendation.

The actual wages, provision of a cottage, clothing and other benefits, will vary so much throughout the country, and will in any event be so rapidly out-dated by inflation, that any actual figures I suggest will be valueless. In practice you will often find it best to start by asking what his present wages and other benefits are. In his reply he will not only tell you what he gets but the improvements he seeks. If possible you should pre-arm yourself by talking to other syndicate organisers about local standards.

Having found your man, the next step is to plan his work in such a way that he operates as effectively as possible but without his feeling that you are interfering unreasonably. This can only be achieved if you know what you are talking about, keep in regular contact with him, and make regular tours of the shoot in which matters of detail are discussed. It may be that he is bright enough to sort out the priorities for himself, but you will be courting trouble if you assume this. Even if your regular involvement makes little difference to what he does it may, at least, affect how he does it for there is nothing like regular visits from the boss to keep a man on his toes. As I commented earlier, there are few jobs where a man can be both left alone for long periods and not asked to show positive results for his time. The ultimate test, of course, is how many pheasants there are on the ground when the season starts. Even this is not conclusive unless you have experience of the ground under another keeper. A good show of birds is not necessarily the optimum for the ground.

The question of managing the keeper's efforts leads conveniently to the important rule that he should have only one boss, for if all the members of the syndicate felt free to instruct the poor man would be in an impossible position. It should be made plain to all members that all but the most simple requests should be channelled through the shoot organiser. Extending the matter of human relations more widely, every effort should be made to further goodwill between the keeper and the men who farm the shoot's land. This is a principle to which homage is always paid, but not every shoot organiser actually does as much about achieving it as he could. I have personal experience of one, very fine shoot on the borders of Suffolk where a state of perpetual war exists between the head keeper and the farm manager which must cost the shoot at least 500 head a season. Nothing but good can come of allowing the farm workers to ferret rabbits, or decoy pigeons, if they wish, and this does not harm the shoot. An occasional brace of pheasants should go to the farmer or his manager, and your keeper should be well aware that if any crisis occurs on the farm he has your full permission to help in every way possible.

At the beginning ensure that your keeper knows the various aspects of the law which affect his work and that you expect him to conform, particularly with regard to the Protection of Birds Act. There are, perhaps, still a few keepers about who are not aware that all hawks and owls are fully protected. There may even be the odd organiser who lets it be known that he will turn a blind eye to the occasional transgression. Such behaviour, if it exists, is a short-sighted disgrace. Of course some gamebirds, mainly chicks, are lost to hawks and owls but this is a modest price to pay for the existence of some very fine birds.

Pole traps are, of course, illegal, as are gin traps. The actual techniques of vermin control are well detailed in the Game Conservancy booklets and elsewhere, and it is pointless to repeat the information here.

As most keepers are practical men and sometimes weak on paper work, it is a wise precaution to check their forward planning. For example, check that space for incubator hatching is reserved, or day-old chicks and rearing food ordered. Nearer the season, inquire if beaters have been engaged, particularly if any of your dates clash with another local shoot.

It is impossible, nor as I explained at the beginning of this chapter am I trying, to cover the whole of the arts of keepering in a few pages. I touch on grouse, partridge and other game in the next chapter and will confine the rest of this one to the three basic aspects of artificially increasing pheasant numbers: rearing, releasing and feeding.

Progress in rearing is shown by the fact that in his excellent book, *Syndicate Shooting*, published in 1961, F. G. Stanfield regarded broodies as the standard way of rearing, but spoke of the great prospects for artificial methods when more was learnt. Rearing with broody hens was a tedious business and seventy coops, producing about 1,000 pheasants, was all one man could manage. With modern equipment it is not unreasonable to expect a single-handed keeper to rear 4,000, which, conveniently, is a sensible number for a good class shoot. Obviously smaller shoots, or those operating on a self-help basis, will want lesser numbers, but the modern principles of rearing will still apply.

The basic principles of modern rearing are now well established, and it is difficult to see change in anything but detail, at least for some years to come. Essentially, eggs are now hatched by incubator, and the chicks reared in heated brooder units. Your problem is to consider your personal circumstances and decide which degree of involvement is best. At one extreme you can simply buy day-olds, and at the other you will catch up your own birds, hatch them in your own incubator and thus avoid payment to an outsider at any stage – all very satisfactory, but leaving no time for your keeper to help the wild stock. A bold organiser, with a business brain, will consider employing extra labour, thereby freeing his keeper for true keepering, rearing more birds than he needs and using the profit from the sale of the surplus to pay for the labour.

The large-capacity brooder units now in use have done away with the old, time-consuming, rearing fields, but some people claim that even more time is saved by intensive indoor rearing. In most cases the birds are moved to outside runs when 3–5 weeks old, but under some systems remain indoors until up to eight weeks old. As I have no personal experience I cannot comment authoritatively but, in principle, I am not happy about any creature developing indoors, and often in lighting which is deliberately dimmed. In particular birds reared partly indoors are more vulnerable when they are eventually released into whatever weather conditions fate hands out to them.

As I write the system of overcoming feather picking by the use of plastic anti-peck bits has only been in popular use for two seasons. However, it has proved so successful that the laborious method of de-beaking appears likely to die out before long.

We come, then, to the question of releasing the poults, and this is of critical importance for all shoots; even more so, if that is possible, for the more modest ones which lack the constant presence of a keeper. Now that the broody/rearing field system has gone, release pens have taken over, and perform the twofold function of keeping predators out and the poults in until they have become acclimatised. The siting of release pens is most important. They must, of course, be in the best coverts and away from the boundaries of the shoot. Sunning areas and roosting cover are essential, and the Game Conservancy recommends a minimum perimeter of a metre per bird up to 100, but reducing for larger numbers until at 1,000 birds 0·3 metres per bird will suffice. Put another way each bird needs about 6 square metres of space. A relatively flimsy structure will keep pheasants in, but it will not keep predators out, and a single fox can kill, some physically and some by sheer fright, several dozen pheasants in a single visit. It is, therefore, foolish not to make a thorough job, which means a minimum height of 2 metres with an extra 0·3 metre turned out at the top. Ideally the bottom should be well dug in, but personally I peg lengths of tree trunks in a continuous barrier.

As the release pen is not roofed it is necessary to restrict the poults' ability to fly until they have settled into their new surroundings. Although brailing is possible I have always found wing clipping both simple and satisfactory. The birds will not be able to flutter out of the pen for some 2–3 weeks, and will then return to feed through one-way tunnels. Although I have never seen it mentioned elsewhere I make a point of building, within the release pens, replicas of the feed points around the shoot. As a result when the birds begin to range further afield they immediately recognise a feed point for what it is. On well-keepered shoots, where the birds will be fed at set times, this has no significance but it is worth following by other shoots. Naturally an adequate supply of water is essential in the pens and, indeed, on the shoot itself, if there is not a natural supply.

Which brings us to the tricky question of foxes. Some interesting and worthy experiments have been carried out in the last few years, which have demonstrated that a pheasant shoot can operate successfully without eliminating every fox, and that shooting can take place successfully only a few days after the coverts have been visited by hounds. I do not dispute these conclusions, but I am anxious that shoots organisers should see the position clearly. Pheasants do not harm foxes, but foxes do harm pheasants – particularly during the breeding season when sitting hens are very vulnerable and young birds easily caught. Additionally, while pheasants unquestionably do return to their home coverts fairly quickly after being disturbed, it is better that they are left in peace. This is not to suggest that I oppose the view that shooting and hunting men should work together – on the contrary I am a great advocate of all field sports making common cause. But the shoot organiser must realise that if there were no other considerations then foxes should be eliminated from the shoot – not to do so is a political rather than a practical decision. Where there is no objection to fox control the arrival of poults in the release pens will attract foxes which can often be snared as they circle the pens searching for a weak spot. The technique of snaring has recently been examined by the Hunting and Shooting Committee of the B.F.S.S. and its conclusions have been set out in a pamphlet 'Code of Conduct for Snaring'.

With the birds reared, and free to roam, the final problem is to keep them on the shoot. The standard answer is to feed them regularly and adequately, but even well-fed birds will not tolerate poor surroundings – time spent early in the year in improving the general habitat will be well repaid. This may have taken the form of planting cover crops, or fencing off unwanted corners to allow rough cover areas, indeed, anything which overcomes the modern game preservers' problem of large fields surrounded by barbed wire.

Feeding techniques will vary according to the resources of the shoot, but whatever they may be it is important to bear in mind the foolishness of rearing pheasants only to allow them to wander away to your better-fed, neighbour's ground. Conversely proper feeding on your part will ensure that any 'foreign' birds entering your ground are likely to stay. (This is not an unneighbourly suggestion, for provided a shoot has put down a reasonable number of birds it is perfectly entitled to make every effort to hold strays.)

The best method of feeding pheasants is to make them hunt for it, which is why the old method of scattering corn on straw rides at regular times, the meanwhile whistling the birds in, remains the best. Unfortunately the time involved makes this well-nigh impossible for shoots without a full-time keeper. The modern alternative is the automatic feeder which scatters predetermined quantities of corn at predetermined times, whilst ringing a bell to summon the pheasants. This is not so good as a good keeper but better than an unreliable one.

Obviously the cost of equipping all the coverts with automatic feeders is quite heavy and will be too much for many smaller shoots. There are various designs of hoppers which only require replenishing at intervals, and these do the job reasonably, but have the disadvantage that the birds can come, eat and go in a short time. As I described earlier I try to compromise by building feed points, which combine both hoppers and dry straw under a roof of corrugated asbestos. When the hoppers are replenished several handfuls of corn can be thrown over the straw, and the birds seem content to scratch away happily even when there is little hope of success. The simplest and best-known form of hopper is the five-gallon drum with slits in the side, lifted beyond the reach of rats and small birds by bricks. A variation is to replace the bottom with a small mesh netting, through which corn will just fall if pecked. The drum is then raised to a height just reachable by a pheasant or partridge. Feed points attract rats and thereby centralise them for a poisoning campaign.

The time at which feeding must begin will vary from shoot to shoot. Those where cereals form an important part of the farm programme will derive little benefit from feeding until the stubbles are ploughed in, whereas others may need to feed immediately the birds begin to leave the release pens.

7

Rough Shooting

Positioning this chapter on rough shooting towards the end of the book is an indication of the complexities of the other forms of game shooting rather than my affection for this form of the sport. Pitting one's wits and dog against a few wily old pheasants on a crisp January day is as absorbing and exciting a sport as anything else in shooting. But, deferred as this chapter may be, its inclusion is confirmation of my earlier point that game shooting involves all form of shooting game.

Although not strictly apposite to the purpose of the book, it is interesting to attempt a definition of precisely what rough shooting is, if only because most authors of books on the subject commence by so doing and rarely agree with one another. The difficulty arises because everyone knows where rough shooting begins but no one is quite sure where it ends. By which I mean that a man and a dog, poking around a piece of rough ground for whatever game God may have put there, are undeniably rough shooting; but are four men with several dogs and a couple of their children beating, who a few months previously released a few dozen pheasants on the ground, also rough shooting?

Other problems of definition arise. It is appealing to apply the rule that in rough shooting all the Guns are mobile; but a pair of knowledgeable rough shooters will frequently operate as a driving/standing team.

Habitat improvement and winter feeding are as important to the rough shoot as the driven and, as I detail later, there is a strong case for rearing birds for a rough shoot. In the chapter 'On a Lesser Scale', I dealt with shoots of lesser complexity and ambition until reaching the level at which the members did all their own keepering and most of their driving. Somewhere between this minor form of driven shooting and the most sophisticated forms of rough shooting there must lie a boundary at which rough shoots and driven shoots are separated.

Whilst of no great consequence for the future of the sport, it is none the less an interesting point and I will suggest a few ground rules. Firstly a rough shoot will not employ a full-time keeper. (I do not think the employment of, for example, a part-timer to carry out winter feeding necessarily takes a shoot out of the rough category.)

Secondly, all the Guns will participate *most* of the time in walking up or driving the quarry. Thirdly, any rearing will be on a modest scale. Finally, the numbers participating will be relatively few. Here, with this point, lies a major argument. At what number does a rough shoot cease to be a rough shoot? It can be contended that provided everyone is actually mobile the numbers are of no consequence, but the thought of a rough shoot with, say, sixteen Guns, is ridiculous. The popular view, I suspect, is that a rough shoot will normally have from one to three and at the most four Guns. Here I disagree. A rough shoot is a combination of the way one pursues the quarry and an attitude of mind. Rough shooters are hunters in the true sense, and if we seek a brief definition this is the real nub of it – rough shooting is hunting the quarry. If this is true then there is theoretically no limitation on the numbers involved. In practice, there is, and for two reasons. Firstly, informality is the very wine of rough shooting and as numbers rise this inevitably fades. Secondly, the art of the game is using your fieldcraft and cunning to outwit the quarry – surround and overpower it by sheer weight of numbers and the sport has evaporated – you might as well take the field in a football match with two dozen men in your team.

So, I repeat my final point that the numbers participating will be relatively few. Relative to what? To the ground. If the shoot is mainly hedges two men are enough; if it is endless acres of Forestry Commission woodland, eight or even ten will not destroy the essential character of a rough shoot.

Which is quite enough on this aspect in a book concerning itself with economies and organisation, except for the comment that present problems are likely to see an increase in rough shooting and, with it, the number of dogs working hard rather than spending the great bulk of their time sitting by a peg. And a good job too.

Any reader wishing to learn more about the actual mechanics of rough shooting has an excellent choice of suitable books, of which one of the latest and best is Arthur Cadman's *Guide to Rough Shooting*, published in 1974.

The degree of economies and organisation involved will vary enormously with the ground. The man with a large slice of Scottish moor, far from any big towns, and with a natural supply of game has no problems. His southern contemporary, pestered by poachers, vermin, intensive farming practices and competition from other sportsmen offering the landlord higher rent, has.

The major difficulty, as always, is finding the ground. This is intensified as the demand for lower-priced sport is obviously greater than higher. Shortage of local tenants frequently forces the owner of a large formal shoot to advertise it widely, but rough shoots rarely appear in the sporting press advertisement columns. This makes it all the more necessary for potential tenants to insert their own 'wanted' advertisements, and also to take the initiative in other ways. Personal contact is by far the best method, but this is of little help to those with limited rural contacts. Pigeon shooting is often an entrée, for when pigeons are damaging crops an offer to decoy is often welcome. Building on this relationship can lead to a good opportunity.

It is a mistake to expect to find rough shooting at a lower rent per acre than driven. You may be fortunate, but the pressure for small rough shoots is so great that the rent can often be higher than for driven. Having found a possible shoot, virtually all the advice given in the second chapter on the desirable qualities applies. Unfortunately so does the overriding fact that even if the ground is poor you will rarely have a choice. The need for a lease is no less for a rough shoot than a driven shoot – indeed, it is probably greater, for driven tenants are not so frequently bothered by competitors offering higher rents. Regrettably landlords on smaller shoots are more inclined to treat this aspect casually, and often prefer merely to exchange letters or rely on verbal agreement. You stand in a weak position but if possible persuade him to have a written lease for a sensible term. It is likely that in seeking the ground you will have offered the carrot of wishing to improve the shooting. If you are to spend time and money doing this it is reasonable that you should hold some reasonable security of tenure.

Having found ground it is only common sense to go to considerable trouble to stay on good terms with the owner. Even a long lease eventually ends, and most owners will prefer a well-known and liked existing tenant to a higher rent offered by a rival. Wilson Stephens recently suggested that the arrival of the deep freeze had brought to an end the era of giving presents of game or fish. Perceptive as all his writings are, it would be a foolish tenant who failed to see his landlord well provided for.

The belief that rough shooters are by nature men who prefer their own company – a form of inland wildfowler – is often erroneous. Finance and a desire to hunt the quarry naturally, often stimulated by a love of working dogs, are the more usual influences. Assuming a prospective rough shooter is not anti-social, the scope of his activities can be greatly extended by joining with companions. Obviously the more men share the cost, the more ground can be leased, and the more effort put into its improvement. Some will object on the basis that although the bag will be larger it will be shared by more Guns, and an individual's personal sport will not be improved. At the same time the more men involved the greater the complexities, and the further the venture moves from the desirable simplicity of a rough shoot. The first point I believe to be inaccurate, for the combined efforts and money of several men should produce a greater average bag per man than those of one or two men. On the second I can only observe that it depends on individuals and, as I pointed out earlier, on the ground. From a purely personal viewpoint I prefer to do my rough shooting with only a few companions. The probability is that most readers will feel the same, but I would be negligent in not pointing out the opportunities that a larger union can bring. In fact in some areas it may be essential to do this to achieve the purchasing power necessary to produce the ground.

Once found, most ground will be capable of considerable improvement, that is from the shooting tenant's viewpoint. Again it is essential to seek the owner's permission, and this is more likely to be given if you explain not only what you want to do, but why. Many rough shoots are rough in name only, and if intensively farmed will be desperately short of nesting and winter cover. Most farms have odd rough corners, unfarmable bankings, areas between pylons, and similar patches from which stock can be fenced and suitable, low, permanent cover planted. Broom is good, and the seeds can be readily gathered from wild plants. In the early stages old wire netting and similar 'scaffolding' can be deposited to enable the natural grass and weed growth to stand through the winter.

It is unlikely that either the lease or finances will permit the growth of annual cover crops, but if there is a central and unused area a special game mixture is not expensive and attracts pheasants from a wide area.

Winter feeding is, of course, critical and all the advice given in Chapter 6 applies. In particular, note the suggestion that corn should be taken to central points early in the season before wet ground conditions make transport difficult.

At one time few rough shoots reared pheasants but the practice is now extensive. How much this is due to an awakening social conscience and how much to modern, time-saving, rearing equipment and techniques, it is impossible to say, but the trend is very welcome. From the tenant's angle sensible rearing will mean more sport, and more pleasurable involvement during a longer period of the year. From a neighbour's angle it ends the sharp practice of, effectively, stealing his birds by letting him rear them and then enticing them with food near the boundary. I stress, sensible rearing, for the problems of rearing and most important, retaining birds are even harder for the rough shoot than the driven. The latter will have regular help, whereas the rough shooter usually has to sandwich his keeping in between all life's other demands. Rearing obviously creates the greatest problems for the amateur, for whereas with most keepering activities it is of little consequence whether they are performed at a given hour, or even on a given day, young pheasants must have regular attention. This requirement will probably eliminate rearing on the shoot but, as explained previously, home rearing is perfectly feasible, although much easier if undertaken from the day-old stage. Beginners to rearing should bear in mind that the well-organised man has done a great deal of the work before the day-olds actually arrive. There is a surprising amount of work involved in either building or renovating rearing and release pens, disinfecting equipment, stocking with food, and generally preparing. It is sensible to complete this in good time and avoid a last-minute rush. In fact I find I spend more hours in preparation in the weeks before the chicks arrive than I do in the subsequent weeks of feeding and watering.

Remember particularly my advice on keeping very young birds warm. In the early stages they chill very easily, and are surprisingly stupid about learning to use the heat source in the brooder house. If the weather is cold during the first few days after hatching it is better to keep the chicks confined to the brooder house than run the risk of their chilling. At this stage the degree of outdoor freedom they are allowed should depend on their supervision. If you are fortunate enough to have a wife or relative who is good at these things there are few problems, but if birds have to be left alone for several hours at a stretch it is best to show caution. My wife is now an expert at reviving apparently dead, chilled pheasant chicks, which she does by the drastic process of placing them in the oven, set at low heat!

In practice, you are as likely to lose birds from trampling as chilling, for when they feel cold chicks tend to pack together in a corner of the run rather than seek the heat in the brooder house. Instinct drives them to huddle together in a form of avian rugby match, and unless the human referee breaks up the scrum quickly, the bottom layer will be dead. The secrets of successful rearing are careful preparation, good management and constant vigilance.

Although most rough shooters do their own rearing and keepering there is no reason why, given the finance, a part-time keeper should not be employed. Most men would rather have good-quality rough shooting than poor-quality driven and, for a given sum of money it is easier to provide the former than the latter. Consider, for example, how many more pheasants can be put down with the money otherwise spent on beaters. There are many variations of expenditure and personal labour and my purpose is not to attempt to convert readers to any particular plan, but to encourage them to think deeply of the alternatives open.

Organisation is obviously a far simpler matter than in driven shoots, a fact which may explain why so many shoot organisers enjoy rough shooting. The aim of a shooting day moves from contriving the smooth synchronisation of men and machines essential to a large driven day, to directing one's cunning to outwitting the quarry. There are many excellent books on this aspect of shooting and, in any event, it is outside the scope of this one. However, organisation involves planning in advance, and under this head comes any work necessary to facilitate tactics on a shooting day. Only experienced rough shooters know how rapidly pheasants will travel on foot and unless they are carefully and quietly cut off only a small percentage of the birds on the ground will be cornered. Arthur Cadman puts it well in his book, 'The human voice travels a long way. A cock pheasant will travel further, very quickly.' Success will be easier if obvious escape routes are removed or blocked well in advance. For example, with permission a short hedge connecting two areas of thick cover can be cleared, or a wire netting barrier erected. The newcomer to rough shooting tends to think it is a fairly simple matter of walking through suitable cover with dogs and shooting that which flushes. This plan possibly works well in October with young, inexperienced game about, but by January sport is likely to be extremely dull. The art of rough shooting is getting in range of the quarry, which means not only finding it, but so arranging matters that it cannot slip away out of range. This calls for a thorough knowledge of the ground and careful preliminary planning. However, it is essential to be flexible and, if necessary, vary the plan for the day to take account of changed conditions. An alert mind and eye are needed to get the best results.

As with driven shooting, common sense will once again dictate that the day starts on the boundaries and cover is worked in towards the centre of the shoot.

Water on the shoot is of great value to rough shooters for, apart from helping to hold pheasants, it offers great shooting potential. Low, wet areas may hold snipe, and the comments in the next chapter on improving snipe habitat may be useful. Ponds, lakes and rivers will nearly always have a duck population, and this can be improved, sometimes dramatically, by feeding with wheat, barley or potatoes. However the business of developing and shooting a flight pond should be carried out with discretion. From a practical angle, if it is shot more frequently than every three weeks or so the duck will be frightened off. From a wider angle, flight ponds can be very effective, and it is not ethical to draw in and slaughter too many duck from the surrounding countryside.

It hardly needs recording that my previous comments on the need for insurance against accidents apply as much to rough shoots as driven. Although there are fewer people involved the lack of formality in the proceedings creates more potentially dangerous situations.

8

Grouse, Partridge and other Game

So far this book has concentrated almost entirely on pheasants – an unromantic but realistic approach, for the elimination of the pheasant from many shoots would leave little else. Many shooting men will feel that relegating the other species to second place is wrong and, taking a general view, I agree wholeheartedly. Unfortunately when men are paying a considerable sum of money for sport (and £100 is as considerable to a man of lesser means as £1,000 is to others) they do not take a general view, but the very specific one of wanting a sufficient volume of shooting. Only after they are satisfied in terms of quantity will they look for variety, and the hard fact is that the pheasant is the most reliable and economic sporting quarry.

This said, however, there is both a duty on shooting men to encourage other species and a considerable reward from the variety that ensues. In this chapter I want to look briefly at the position with and the prospects for other game.

The grouse is probably in the happiest position. Its habitat is such that the pressures brought about by an excess of human beings are unlikely to affect it. (I write these words on the Isle of Mull, looking at a wide vista of hills which disappear, re-appear and then vanish once more under curtains of hail, driven by a force 9 gale. Somewhere in the blizzard large numbers of grouse, ptarmigan and red deer are surviving in conditions which would kill most humans in a few hours. Apart from the traditional interference that occurs from 12 August onward mankind leaves them in peace.) Compared to reared pheasants, grouse are relatively cheap to provide, if one ignores the capital cost of the ground. The subject is somewhat complex, but much pheasant shooting takes place on ground purchased on its agricultural merit and the shooting is something of a bonus, whereas many moors have been purchased principally on their sporting potential, and a true costing of the shooting has to include an interest element for the capital tied up. Theoretically hard times should hit both grouse and pheasant shooting equally, but the indications are that grouse shooting is suffering far less. There are, I think, two reasons.

Firstly, it is an easy matter for a pheasant shoot to save money by simply rearing fewer pheasants. A grouse moor, however, cannot rear fewer grouse and, short of just not shooting, the only obvious step is the drastic one of selling the moor to recover capital. There is not a strong market for grouse moors in conditions of financial recession so most owners will carry on, although some will let more or all of the shooting days.

Which leads to the second reason. Grouse shooting is very popular with visitors from overseas, many of whom are not experiencing our difficulties. Even if they are, they will first drop pheasant shooting in this country, for whereas pheasants can be shot in many countries grouse are indigenous to Britain.

Apart from vermin control most of the labour costs on a moor go to heather burning and driving. The latter is usually heavier than the beating costs for a pheasant shoot, as more men are required. On marginal moors the effect may be a swing away from driving the grouse to dogging them. Overdone this could be a disaster, for while it is claimed that it is impossible to over-shoot a moor by driving, good and persistent dogging is much too efficient. Sensibly restrained, however, the trend has advantages. This particularly attractive form of dog work will receive a boost and the health of the Guns should benefit.

I wish I could write so cheerfully of the partridges. The decline of these attractive birds has continued for so many years now that many men who have come to shooting since the last war have never known a good patridge drive. It is difficult now to realise that at one time some shoots concentrated on partridges and the pheasants were incidentals, while good partridge keepers were regarded as the élite of their profession. *The Partridge*, published in 1893, in the excellent 'Fur and Feather' series contains statistics that illustrate the abundance of partridges in the last century. On the Holkham estate in north Norfolk, the partridge bag for 1855 was 8,100, and in 1887 on Lord Londesborough's Yorkshire estate, the total for one week was 2,311. The records for The Grange, Lord Ashurton's Hampshire estate, are fairly comprehensive. The best week in 1891, which is described as a bad breeding year, yielded 'only' 1,432 partridges, but the two best weeks of 1892 produced 2,324 and 2,422. The record was an October week of 1887 with a bag of 4,109. Of particular interest to me, as I know the ground well, are the figures for the Six Mile Bottom estate. The record week was in January 1869, with a bag of 1,999. The author, A. Stuart-Wortley, goes on to comment that no hares are mentioned, 'for the reason that they were absolutely insignificant in numbers'. He concludes that the great authorities on partridges, whether owners or keepers, regard hares as a bad thing for gamebirds. The significance is that later in this chapter I mention taking part in the record hare shoot when over 1,000 were killed in a day. This was held over the Six Mile Bottom estate – times have indeed changed.

The ground still holds good numbers of partridges but pheasants form by far the greater part of the bag.

These enormous bags were, of course, achieved when neither labour nor expenses were limited, but it is highly unlikely that any of the estates, if indeed they survive in their original form, could repeat those results, even given the same facilities, without changing their present farming techniques. There is no simple reason for the decline, but unquestionably the root cause is changes in agricultural practices. As the extent of the collapse became apparent many people advanced reasons, but, while most suggestions had an element of truth, none were more than informed guesswork until the Game Conservancy started its partridge research project in 1969. The results have been well documented, and most shooting men are aware that partridge chick survival depends mainly upon the abundance or otherwise of insects at the critical time of hatching. The statistical proof is that from 1968 onwards nearly 70 per cent of all variations in chick survival on well-keepered areas could be attributed to variations in insects in cereals. Obviously the extensive use of insecticides is a major cause of the decline but a lesser-known factor is the herbicides which kill the homes or scaffolding of the insects. Apart from spraying, the other great detrimental influence of modern farming comes from the cessation of undersowing, and as spraying will not cease, the restoration of partridge numbers in many areas must depend on a restoration of this practice. Hopefully, there are signs of a trend in this direction. Stubble burning also appears to be detrimental, although it is difficult to see quite why as the insect numbers should have recovered by the following spring.

The work of the Conservancy has both confirmed some beliefs and thrown doubt on others. For example, winter losses appear not to be as great as feared, and the reduction in apparent numbers seems to be due to dispersal and not death. Conversely all the old keepers' views about vermin seem confirmed, with the evidence that nesting losses from predators can be very high indeed. In fact the Conservancy conclude that virtual complete removal of foxes and carrion crows is essential, although making the point that in many areas the elimination of foxes may not be desirable. This authoritative statement should be considered in conjunction with my earlier comment on foxes.

High pheasant densities are detrimental to partridges, which become caught in a vicious circle. As their numbers dropped through changes in farming, shoots reared more pheasants. These competed with the partridges for both food and nesting cover, resulting in a further drop in partridge numbers, whereupon the shoots produced more pheasants, and so on. Finally keepers, labouring under the burden of increased pheasant rearing, became less efficient vermin controllers and, as the work of Dr. G. R. V. Potts, the Head Partridge Biologist of the Game Conservancy, has shown, vermin are responsible for major losses among partridge chicks.

From all this, it is obvious that the shoot organisers, struggling to provide reasonable sport in times of high inflation, will be chary of gambling money on partridges. However, as much for the sake of the partridges as the Guns, there is a good case for trying. It is unreasonable to expect the farmer to vary his methods and the only practical measure is rearing, but it is important to appreciate that, due to the peculiarities of reared partridges, the prime object must be to increase the breeding stock rather than this year's bag. While partridges can be released for shooting in much the same way as pheasants, current indications are that the recovery rate will be poor, and the best results will be obtained by keeping them through the winter and releasing them as breeding pairs in the spring. It is not a short term project. The Game Conservancy's booklet no. 4 covers the subject fully.

It is not possible, at least at this time, to improve the numbers of the remaining game species by rearing, but very often an increase can be achieved by improving the habitat. Snipe are a good example. In the autumn and winter months their numbers are greatly boosted by migration from north-west Europe and shoots which take measures to increase suitable habitat will obviously benefit. Snipe shooting was once a popular sport in its own right, but nowadays they tend to be treated as a casual extra in a bigger programme. This is perhaps a sign of the syndicate philosophy that has developed, where the cry is for ever-more pheasants over static Guns, and if events bring about a resurgence of interest in the minor game species this will be a healthy trend. Personally I have had many enjoyable days walking up snipe in the Hebrides which I would not have exchanged for driven pheasants.

If you are fortunate in having on your ground one or more small areas which are slow to freeze, these will attract snipe, often in large numbers, when the surrounding countryside freezes. Failing this happy situation much can be done to improve any existing low, wet ground. The snipe's food is mainly invertebrates, which it seeks by probing with its long beak in soft earth. Consequently the need is for ample areas of permanently soft earth, which is rich in earthworms and other suitable food. Both open, exposed feeding areas and areas choked with thick growth are disliked – the ideal has small open patches of soft ground set among sheltering reeds or rushes. Where the ground is overgrown, patches should be cleared by burning or 'swiping'. A further improvement particularly where the ground is inclined to harden in dry weather, is the creation of small craters, either by hand digging or blasting with small explosive charges. In the latter case the edges must be shelved by hand.

Many of the best snipe areas are created by farm animals, which both cut up the ground and enrich it with manure. It is believed that in the old days artificial manuring of the snipe areas was carried out with blood and offal, but few experiments in this direction have been carried out in this country. Experiments of this nature, and the general improvement of snipe habitat, are very suitable activities for self-help shoots. With a formal syndicate it is hardly possible to divert the efforts of an already hard-worked keeper to snipe without the pheasants suffering, but, in any shoot where the members take a hand, snipe habitat improvement should be both interesting and rewarding. So little is known about this aspect of shooting conservation that any clear results, negative as well as positive, should be reported to other shooting men by way of the correspondence columns of the sporting press.

Woodcock also belong in the class of sporting birds whose numbers are augmented from north-west Europe; in fact, migration accounts for the majority of British woodcock. Unfortunately woodcock share with snipe the problem that modern agricultural practices often destroy their suitable habitat. With snipe the craze to drain has eliminated many boggy areas, and with woodcock modern afforestation provides unsuitable conditions. It is simpler to create fresh habitat for snipe than woodcock, for the former can usually be accommodated in rough, low corners that have little agricultural value, whereas ground suitable for planting with ideal woodcock cover can equally well carry more profitable tree species. Nor can the expenditure of sufficient money ensure good woodcock shooting, for they migrate along narrower and more clearly defined flyways than snipe, and unless a shoot is fortunately positioned no amount of habitat improvement will attract migrants. (Although such work will increase the number of permanently resident birds.)

For those shoots that enjoy a seasonal fall of woodcock there are various measures possible to improve the habitat, but whether it is economical or not will depend on local circumstances. If the potential numbers of woodcock are high, and pheasants do not take kindly to the area, an owner will be more disposed to making the effort than if the woodcock migration is patchy and pheasants are a reliable mainstay. For example, woodcock like comparatively little ground cover, but it would be a foolish man who lost his pheasants by clearing his bramble and other low cover. Woodcock which enter coverts from above, as distinct from pheasants which come in by the side doors as it were, like a broken overhead canopy. Here, work done for one species will benefit another, for clearing open spaces will promote ground growth and sunning areas within coverts for pheasants. Specialised woodcock keepers, of whom there are now very few left, believe that complete quiet is an essential for woodcock and object to the presence of pheasants. Unfortunately, although I am sure that much more will be learnt about the woodcock and the measures necessary to help it, I fear that it will always be the Cinderella to the pheasant. This is inevitable as long as it competes for the same cover. The snipe, on the other hand, is not only happy with open areas but the preservation, and even enlargement, of these areas actually provides more nesting cover for pheasants and partridges.

We come now to one of my favourite gamebirds, the ptarmigan, but I have never shot one and I do not expect I ever will. They are rarely found below the 2,000 feet level, and I am fascinated by these remarkable birds which choose to live in such severe conditions. Only those readers who have actual experience of the hills at these heights will be aware just how very arduous conditions can be and, even then, our experience is confined mainly to the periods of better weather. Their ability to survive the winter in such barren surroundings wins my admiration. Presumably because humans are a rare sight ptarmigan are frequently tame, and I see little achievement in shooting a bird which is prepared to sit and fix one with a curious stare from ten paces. They can, of course, also provide very testing shots, and I have vivid memories of one tearing past my head at 3,000 feet on Blaven in the Cuillins of Skye, but I have no desire to pursue them other than with a camera.

Naturally enough no research has been done on improving the habitat of the ptarmigan. Even if such a study was economically justifiable it is difficult to see what benefit would ensue. The birds themselves could improve their habitat enormously by just decending 1,000 feet or so. If they choose to live among rock and sparse, stunted vegetation there seems little point in improving their surroundings, for they would presumably then depart for some other inferior spot.

If this book were being written for Continental readers I would not only have to mention the hare, but devote an entire chapter to it. In our relative indifference to the hare we British mirror the attitude that, until recently, we showed towards roe deer, which we either ignored or treated as vermin. At last the work of the British Deer Society and the attitude of the Continentals has brought an appreciation of our good fortune, but it is doubtful if we will see a similar swing in favour of hare shooting. Perhaps our attitude stems from the facts that shooting ground game at formal shoots is often frowned on as dangerous, and rough shooters find hares a burden to carry. Personally, I like the occasional hare both for the variety it brings to the shoot and the tasty meal it gives later. Large-scale hare shoots are not, however, for me. I took part in the record Cambridgeshire shoot that produced over 1,000 in a day and found no pleasure in it. This was not a sporting occasion but purely an agricultural operation, comparable with spraying a crop to rid it of an excess of insects.

Although a shoot can be managed to benefit the hares it is not practical so to do. Your ground either has a reasonable number of hares or it has not. If it has I suggest you do not disregard them, but organise the occasional drive specifically for the hares. The value of a quarry is very much, like beauty, in the eye of the beholder, as witness the difference in attitude between stalking red deer stags and hinds. Because you can take his antlers back to the south, men pay large sums to stalk the former but thinning the hinds is left to the stalker and his men, although the skill and energy required is the same. If, by judicious words, a shoot organiser can elevate the status of the hare, some good sport can be had and a pheasant drive or two preserved for another day.

9

Of General Concern

Although the general pattern of game shooting remains the same the changing circumstances of recent years have given rise to several points of interest and concern.

One, of particular concern to all shoot organisers, is the perennial question of safety. The rules are well known and, in a book of this nature, there is no point in repeating them. Space can, however, be justified in looking at the special problems of the present day and, in particular, three distinct aspects which involve shoot organisers.

Half a century ago most of the Guns at a formal shoot would be countrymen by birth and upbringing, even if they spent their working lives in towns. Their apprenticeship in the shooting field would have followed a fairly set pattern, and their early appearances would have been supervised by knowledgeable men. All of us have read the awe-inspiring tales of fierce hosts, dressing down a Gun who has offended the rules of safety and dispatching him from the field. Personally I view these slightly synically, as I suspect the wrath was in inverse proportion to the position of the offender. The distant nephew, who was lucky to have received an invite anyway, was doubtless given no quarter, but an offence by a social superior might go conveniently unobserved. True or not, most men knew how they should behave and most hosts were able and willing to enforce the rules.

Nowadays we have, in most shoots, a different situation, for many of the Guns lack the right experience, and the power of the man in charge to take them to task is less. The problem often begins when the organiser is recruiting Guns for, with costs rising and so many men hard-pressed financially, it is sometimes difficult to raise a full team. An organiser already committed to an expensive lease, and with the other expenses of a shoot looming, may not inquire too closely into a potential member's safety record. If the man seems pleasant, and he has the money, the temptation is to accept him and sigh with relief. Understandable as this is it is unquestionably wrong. A man who sets out to organise a syndicate shoot brings on to his shoulders a moral responsibility to watch over the safety of all concerned, from Guns to the youngest beater. Doing the job for no personal reward is no excuse – the organiser is morally, if not legally, responsible. This obligation does not, however, free the other guns from playing their part – safety is everybody's concern, embarrassing though its enforcement may be.

The second aspect is the need for the man in charge of a shoot to be positive and direct over safety. On a number of occasions I have been present but not in charge when a minor safety offence has been committed. Everyone who has witnessed it will report it to everyone who has not but nothing will be done. The party offended will not lodge a formal complaint to either the offender or the organiser, and the latter, although aware of the incident, does not tackle the situation firmly. It is too embarrassing. This is very wrong, for we are concerned with people's lives and the organiser has a clear duty to act whether he is asked to or not. Frequently the man who escaped has not complained through reluctance to put the organiser in a difficult position – this too is wrong. In the interests of all, including the offender who has scared someone today but may kill someone next week, if a Gun makes a mistake he should be quietly told what has happened and requested to be more careful. If he then commits another crime he should go. The safety rules of shooting really are extremely simple, and any competent person can grasp them quickly. Anyone who consistently offends is more likely to be temperamentally unsound than stupid and, as such, is better shooting alone.

The varied background of modern shooting men makes it necessary for a shoot organiser to spell out the procedure clearly. It is dangerous to assume that all the Guns will know they must empty their guns as soon as 'all out' is called, or that they will automatically check for pickers-up behind before the drive begins. These, and similar instructions, should be given at the start – few men will now consider you fussy.

A year or so ago there was a spate of correspondence in *The Field* on whether Guns, chatting before or after a drive, should have their guns open or closed. The traditionalists argued that no man would have a loaded gun at these times, and insisting that he prove the fact would be offensive. This attitude, whilst admirable in its Christian-like faith in others, is based upon the era now past. Personally, I believe that the overwhelming majority of shooting men are safe but that the very occasional one is not and, rather than take the chance that he has somehow crept into my party, I prefer to see all guns open. This rule is a great help in the difficult situation that arises when a previously safe Gun grows old and forgetful. In particular I knew one man, of great intelligence and ability, who tragically contracted a brain disease and could never recall whether his gun was loaded or empty, or even on safe or not. Once I saw him blow a hole in the ground close to his own feet and mutter, 'I could have sworn it wasn't loaded.' Yet because it had never been the practice of the shoot to have 'open' guns, no one liked to suggest it at this time.

On the matter of safety the modern need, I repeat, is for the man in charge to take a firm line. A few Guns may feel resentful but the majority will be grateful.

Others may not agree with me but, moving briefly from safety to good manners, I believe it is also the responsibility of the organiser to correct a Gun who is consistently guilty of 'poaching' other men's birds. Uncorrected, this is one of the relatively trivial happenings in a shoot which can eventually lead to a bad atmosphere.

The third aspect calling for the special interest of the organiser is what might be called positive, as distinct from negative, safety measures. Positive measures comprise steps taken in advance to prevent a dangerous situation arising, and this means looking at drives from the safety as well as the sporting angle. As a simple illustration: when we took the lease of the Yorkshire grouse moor, mentioned earlier, I found a butt on one drive was out of line with its neighbours. This was obviously unsafe, and I tackled the keeper, who replied that it had stood there over half a century as the ground was too soft in the correct position. So it was, but we hurled in a lot of rock and eventually created a firm base. Over the years I have encountered many drives which are less safe than others, and some of them could be remedied with only minor changes. For instance, on steep ground a lower Gun, firing upwards at what would normally be a safe angle, may be shooting too close to his higher neighbour. A small alteration to the position might place the vulnerable Gun safely over the crest of the hill. Or a stop might be repositioned to a point where he can do his job as effectively but be less exposed. The greatest scope for such safety planning must lie with new shoots, but some very old-established shoots may be unthinkingly carrying on less than perfect procedures.

Next, and properly befitting the title of this chapter, 'Of General Concern', we come to the quality of birds, by which I mean how high and fast our pheasants fly. It is not often that anyone writes something new on the subject of shooting but as the last major development in the weaponry took place in the nineteenth century perhaps this is not entirely the fault of shooting authors. However, occasionally a new situation develops by slow degrees and, although recognised at local levels, is not assessed as a national problem until a writer points out the obvious. We have to thank James Bouskell, and *The Field*, for the article he wrote in 1973 which demonstrated how badly quality had been sacrificed for quantity on many shoots, and how, unless more experienced shooting men took a firm line, what had once been regarded as poorly shown birds could become the norm. The effect was heartening, as correspondent followed correspondent in deploring the trend, although I often wondered how many followed Bouskell's advice that on a shoot of poor birds one should stand by with an empty gun, and allow them free passage. Support, I imagined, would come mainly from those favoured with a surplus of shooting invitations.

Condemning low birds is relatively easy – producing high, fast ones is not. To a large extent your ground determines the quality of the birds, but there are various measures which will bring improvements. A modern problem is that agriculture now takes priority over sport, and cover, either temporary or permanent, cannot always be best placed for showing good pheasants. However, where you have a choice use it to the best advantage; always remember that high birds are invariably good birds. If you cannot put the cover higher consider whether you can place the Guns lower, even if it means taking a drive in another direction.

In permanent woods avoid letting the birds run through, in advance of the beaters, to the edge and rising from there. Clear the ground cover from the last 25 yards or so, or place a wire netting barrier well inside the wood, so that birds will rise well before the edge. A pheasant can produce only so much power, and with this it can either rise rapidly or accelerate quickly – not both. Forced to flush well inside the wood it must first rise to above tree height before putting on speed, whereas those rising at the edge will often concentrate on speed alone. Older birds are stronger birds, and stronger birds fly higher and faster. With this fact so obvious, it is surprising that so many shoots begin before October is out, have their biggest bags in November and by January are chasing a few cocks which, being older and stronger, prove fine sport. It is true that experience plays a part in their performance, but even birds of the year that have been little shot are far better fliers in January than October. This being so there is a very strong case for starting to shoot later and finishing later. You can, after all, shoot them only once and if later pheasants are harder to hit then there are more left for next time. Later shooting also means the leaf is off and the pheasants, seeing the Guns rather sooner, have both greater time and incentive to rise.

All or some of these measures may be possible, according to the individual shoot, but there is one simple rule which is available to all yet so rarely followed – *stand the Guns well back*. This not only gives the birds time to rise and put on speed, but increases the space between the Guns and eliminates the situation where they are so close that poaching is almost inevitable.

Another phenomenon of our time is the growth of sporting agencies and their increasing strength and activity is worth noting, partly for general interest, and partly because they present opportunities for occasional good sport for those who have to take their major luxuries in small doses. It is not unreasonable to suggest that much of the shooting and fishing advertised for short lets by agencies has not been of good quality. In many cases the ground has been regarded simply as a source of income by the owners, and the tenants themselves, having no enduring interest, have shown no discrimination over what or how much has been shot. Results have often been disappointing, and the impression has grown that owners keep the good ground for themselves and let the rest through the agencies. This was no doubt often true, but changed times mean that some very good shoots, never previously sullied by outsiders, are now available for brief lets, and there are others which have been let to carefully vetted tenants where the vetting is no longer so rigorous. As a result men who cannot afford a high-class syndicate Gun, but wish for the occasional good day or so, should find better value for money than in the past.

It is a fallacy to think that all the best driven shooting handled by the agencies is snapped up by wealthy foreigners. This is largely true when applied to grouse for, as I mentioned earlier, if foreigners want to shoot grouse they must come to Britain, but we have no monopoly of good pheasant shooting and, as labour is cheaper in some parts of Europe, the sport they offer is better value. This fact, coupled with the failing world economy having reduced the number of wealthy foreigners as effectively as it has reduced the number of wealthy Englishmen, means overseas pressure for pheasant shooting is not too heavy and better opportunities are now available. With grouse, in the early part of the season, overseas sportsmen take up some 65–70 per cent of the places, although this drops to about 50 per cent as the season progresses and they have their home sport available. The Americans, French, Belgians and Danes are the most common visitors, with the Germans showing more enthusiasm for sport with the rifle.

For us impecunious English there is good value to be had in grouse shooting in October. By then the foreigners, and our own few surviving wealthy sportsmen, have creamed off the sport and departed, and moor owners, anxious to reduce any over-large stocks, are prepared to accept reasonably low rents for a few days. Together with a few friends I have had some really grand days of driven grouse shooting each October, at a Cumberland sporting hotel, although such sport carries the risk that its availability depends upon a good breeding season.

A few enterprising sporting agencies have now gone beyond simply introducing the tenant and landlord to one another and collecting their fee. To cater for the wealthy foreigner they offer a complete service, which includes booking the hotel accommodation, organising the travelling arrangements, obtaining the Game Licence and even providing the cartridges. One man I know, of great resource, has advanced to the stage where he acts as the shoot organiser, although obviously charging a fee over and above his agency fee.

A further refinement is for the agent to rent the shooting personally for a specific period, and then arrange for his own shooting party of paying Guns. This was obviously more attractive when the heavy demand made success fairly certain, but now the agents, understandably, prefer to put the risk back on to the owners.

Finally, what of the future? In this book I have dwelt very briefly on the past and extensively on the present. It would be cowardly not to look ahead.

As long as men are allowed to, and possibly even if they are not, they will pursue game with the same enthusiasm that you and I know so well. The weapons with which we shoot are unlikely to change, for any attempt to improve their efficiency, so that success stems from a mechanical device and not the sportsman's skill, will be unacceptable. Given that the bulk of the land remains in private hands, and that sporting rights are not proclaimed a public right, the quarries should endure. In fact the key to the future of game shooting is, or so I believe, almost entirely political. Left alone the shooting world, which loves its gamebirds as much as its sport, will ensure their survival. But if the politicians interfere, whether destructively or what they believe to be constructively, then it would be a rash man who would believe he could predict the outcome.

Economics will, of course, play a major part but, as we have seen over the last few years, economics does not greatly alter game shooting. It changes the emphasis here, remoulds the shape there, and both removes and produces opportunities in various places. But, in the end, nothing much is altered – the real threat is political.

In my view shooting will never be banned in this country. Politicians who, I would mention, I do not feel as badly about as many people, have an impossible job, and are no more inclined to look for unnecessary trouble than the rest of us. Some things they have to do and others, such as banning shooting, they will do if it can be shown to be socially desirable and not unfavourable in terms of winning votes. The outcry from the shooting community when the then Conservative Government produced its Green Paper on the subject of increased restrictions on the ownership and use of shotguns, led to a rapid re-thinking, and a proposal to ban the sport altogether would lead to such a storm of protest that any Government would think twice about proceeding. Apart from the unpopularity they would attract, from all classes, the point arises that any law is a bad law if it cannot be enforced, and it is difficult to see the shooting men of Britain meekly giving up a sport their forefathers have pursued for centuries and which they would believe, with truth, was being denied them by a town-orientated Government.

Our greater threats are not a complete ban, but either legislation against rearing birds for sport, or a socialistically inspired drive to make sporting rights open to all. The first has an emotive appeal to those who know nothing of the sport. Argued out logically there is an excellent case for realising the full potential of land to carry its maximum crop of gamebirds, and this reasoning must carry growing force in a world where the production of food is an ever-increasing problem. It is difficult to argue that it is reasonable to stock land with bullocks and then kill them for profit, but unreasonable also to stock it with pheasants and kill them for pleasure. Both activities produce good food, and the latter makes more use of the natural produce of hedges and trees which would otherwise go to waste.

The moral arguments of whether humans should kill wild creatures for pleasure have all been thrashed out before and will be again – I will not weary you with them. But politically neither case is so conclusive that I see politicians acting. At the end the *status quo*, backed up by the undeniable fact that game is good food, should endure.

Whether we shall see some dreaded free-for-all on sporting rights develop I cannot tell and neither can you. If the events of the last few years have proved anything it is that ours is a frail-world; a man-made contrivance tied together with slender threads, and none of us can forecast which will snap, nor what the consequences will be.

We can but hope, and give thanks for the sport we presently enjoy. For our own sake, for the sake of our children, and for the sake of our beloved game, we must protect it as best we can.

Appendix A

The following booklets are, at the moment of writing, available from the Game Conservancy, Fordingbridge, Hampshire. As they are constantly being revised, and new booklets published, the list and prices will vary from time to time. Details of current booklets can be obtained from the Conservancy.

Game and Shooting Crops   Booklet 2   40p
Wildfowl Management   Booklet 3   20p
Partridge Rearing   Booklet 4   40p
Pheasant Egg Production   Booklet 5   30p
Some Diseases of Gamebirds and Wildfowl   Booklet 6   100p
Farm Hazards to Game   Booklet 7   30p
Pheasant Rearing   Booklet 8   25p
Sex and Age in Gamebirds   Booklet 9   30p
Hatching Gamebirds' Eggs   Booklet 11   40p
Grouse Management   Booklet 12   50p
Forestry and Pheasants   Booklet 15   50p
Enemies of Game   Booklet 16   15p
Roe Deer   Booklet 17   75p
Red-legged Partridges   Booklet 18   35p

Game on the Farm   50p
(This is a digest of most of the above booklets and is a mine of useful advice and information.)

Appendix B

Being a specimen letter from a syndicate organiser to a new Gun, setting out the basis of his membership:

Dear X,

I am pleased to welcome you as a member of the High Standing shoot and hope that you will have many pleasant days with us. You will, I feel sure, wish me to confirm the arrangements existing between you and your fellow Guns.

As I think you know we plan to release 3,500 pheasant poults and, to this end, are purchasing 4,000 day-old chicks. Obviously there can be no guarantee that this target will be achieved but our previous experience is encouraging.

The contribution from each member cannot be established finally until the end of the season but it is expected to be about £1,000. This is due in two payments of £500, one due now and the balance on 1 August. No doubt you will let me have your cheque shortly.

Although I am the shoot manager I derive no personal advantage and perform the duties on the understanding that I carry no greater responsibility than other members. It is a condition of membership that all Guns are equally liable for any problems, financial or otherwise, that may arise.

I confirm that a comprehensive insurance policy is in force which covers the shoot against any accident which may occur and also insures individuals against loss of life or injury. You are welcome to examine the policy if you wish.

Finally, I come to the important question of safety and, as I explained, it is a strict condition of membership that any Gun behaving dangerously can be dismissed from the syndicate. In this unfortunate event if a replacement can be found his subscription, or that part of it which is regained, will be refunded, but if no replacement is obtained the whole subscription will be forfeited.

Please forgive me concluding on such a negative note but no doubt you are equally as anxious as other members that a strict standard of safety should be observed.

We will, as explained, be shooting on ten days and I will send you a complete schedule shortly. This will include details of meeting places and lunch arrangements. Ladies are very welcome, as are dogs, if under control. We do not shoot double guns.

I look forward to meeting you again on the first day of the season.

Yours sincerely,
A. N. ORGANISER

Index

Advertising: for Guns, 45; for keepers, 74; for ground, 27, 81
Anti-peck bits, 70, 77
Ashburton, Lord, 87
Automatic feeders, 66, 78, 79

Bag records, 31
Beaters: alternatives, 42; availability, 31, 64; wages, 22, 42, 71; young, 42, 71
B.F.S.S., 17, 78
Bouskell, James, 95, 96
British Deer Society, 91

Cadman, Arthur, 81, 85
Cats, 70
Charles II, King, 14
Coles, Charles, 8, 16
Compensation, game damage, 34
Corn, feed, 22, 65, 78
Cost analyses, 36
Cover crops, 29, 30, 34, 41, 43, 68, 78, 83
Coverts, 29, 30, 31, 34, 35, 43

Disease, 70
District Valuer, 41

Eley Game Advisory Station, 17
Elveden, 15, 56
Estate agents, 29

Feather picking, 70
Feeding, covert, 41

Field, The, 8, 24, 27, 62, 94, 95
Flight ponds, 85
Flintlock, 15
Forestry Commission, 29, 81
Foxes, 37, 55, 62, 63, 70, 77, 78, 88
Fur and Feather series, 87

Game Conservancy, 16, 35, 36, 41, 66, 69, 70, 73, 77, 88, 89
Gamekeepers' Association, 74
Gamonia or the art of preserving game, 14
George V, King, 15
Germicides, 70
Gin traps, 76
Green Paper, the, 98
Grouse, 86, 87, 97
Guide to Rough Shooting, 81

Half Guns, 50
Hares, 87, 91, 92
Hawker, Col. Peter, 11, 15
Holkham estate, 87

I.C.I. Game Research Station, 16
Incubators, multi-stage, 40
Inflation, 13
'Instant' pheasants, 16, 60
Instructions to Young Sportsmen, 11
Insurance, 24, 47, 85
Iveagh, Lord, 15, 16

Index

Jefferies, Richard, 13

Ladies, 54
Leases, 32, 64, 68, 82
Legal obligations, 46
Londesborough, Lord, 87
Lunch, 55, 56

Manton, Joe, 14
Memoirs of a Gamekeeper, 15

Numbering, 52, 53

Outside days, 53

Partridge, The, 87
Partridges, 87, 88
Part-time keepers, 37, 61, 63, 64, 66, 73, 80, 84
Percussion ignition, 15
Pickers-up, 43, 55
Pigeons, 57, 82
Poaching, 28, 30, 51, 63, 64, 81
'Poaching', 95
Pole traps, 76
Potts, G. R. V., Dr., 89
Poults, cost of, 38, 62, 63, 65
Protection of Birds Act, 75
Ptarmigan, 86, 91

Rain, 57
Rates, sporting, 21, 41

Red deer, 86, 92
Release pens, 77
Rents, shooting, 21, 31, 41, 60, 82
Ripon, Lord, 15
Roe deer, 91

Safety, 46, 47, 71, 93, 94
Selling game, 43
Shooting Times, The, 8, 26, 27
Singh, Maharajah Duleep, 65
Six Mile Bottom, 87
Snipe, 85, 89, 90, 91
Sporting agencies, 96, 97
Sportsman's Bag, 9, 59
Stanfield, F. G., 73, 76
Stephens, Wilson, 8, 82
Stops, 47, 52, 71
Stuart-Wortley, A., 87
Subscriptions, 48
Substitute Guns, 48
Syndicate Shooting, 73, 76

Tenant farmers, 31, 67
Tipping, 56
Transport, 36, 41
Turner, Tommy, 15, 16, 56

VAT, 24

WAGBI, 17, 74
Wet areas, 30, 85, 89
Wing-tags, 69
Woodcock, 90, 91